Rudolf Steiner's First Class Verses

A new translation with commentary

Adrian Anderson PhD

Threshold Publishing, Australia, 2018
www.rudolfsteinerstudies.com

Distributed by Ebooks Alchemy
Prahran VIC 3181
Australia

© 2019 A. Anderson

The author asserts the moral right to be regarded as
the originator of this book

ISBN 978-0-648135845 (paperback)

ISBN 978-0-648135852 (hardback)

Contents

Foreword

Illustrations

Other books by Adrian Anderson

Website

Foreword

The First Class Lessons are the deepest and most esoteric instruction sessions for the self-initiation path ever given by Rudolf Steiner, a person regarded by experienced students of spiritual wisdom as a high initiate. Hence a prior engagement with anthroposophy over several years and a serious interest in a deeper, esoteric form of meditation is needed to work with these verses, as they are part of an especially deep spiritual wisdom. In 1924 Rudolf Steiner took up the task of providing guidance in deeper meditative work by offering these esoteric lessons to the members of the General Anthroposophical Society. He had already provided such initiatory sessions, from 1904 to 1914, but this had to cease when the First World War began. The 1924 sessions are called the "The First Class Lessons" because he intended to establish a more advanced, 'Second Class' and also an even more advanced, 'Third Class'. But his premature death in March of 1925 meant, tragically, that these additional, higher classes did not come about.

It became clear to me, after working with these verses over a 40-year period, that many of them have nuances in the original German which have never been seen, making the translation of many verses incorrect. A clear understanding of the meaning of the verses is crucial for their right use, but this is not easy to acquire, as Rudolf Steiner has used the German language in remarkable ways in these verses, in his endeavour to present high initiatory experiences in earthly terms.

It also became clear that, at times, there is a second meaning in a mantric verse, a meaning which Rudolf Steiner indicated, even if only briefly, in his commentary or 'Lessons'. This second meaning goes deeper into initiatory knowledge than the surface meaning. Confirmation of the dual nature of the verses is also to be found in his introductory comment that the Lessons were being offered to two groups of listeners. One group, he says, is comprised of those who intend to actually take up the task of self-transformation and experientially tread the path to self-initiation. The other group is comprised of those who are interested seriously in understanding the path to self-initiation, and may perhaps take up the inner discipline, in the future. When I reveal this second layer of meaning, reference will be made to where Rudolf Steiner's comments confirm this.

Rudolf Steiner did not give any requirements or advice as to when, or how, to meditate with these verses; this is left up to the decision of the meditant. However, he gave advice about the general practice of meditating and the resulting spiritual challenges and experiences, to his approximately 1,000 students in the course of some 220 lessons. The notes of his sessions written down by these students, a large amount of which I gathered up in the early 1980's, were used by me to write the book, *The Way to the Sacred.*

Why this book was written

1: To provide a correct version of the 19 verses, removing the numerous errors in the officially sanctioned versions, to help serious meditants to work with what the verses are actually indicating. That these verses have been misunderstood in places, is not surprising given the very complex and subtle nuances in the German originals.

2: The second purpose is to provide a contemplative commentary, offering insights into the meaning of the many obscure phrases and words.[1] Where there is a second, deeper meaning, my commentary also endeavours to make this clear.

---

[1] The two commentaries by S. Prokofieff are not referred to in this book, as they are very different in focus and spirit to what I'm presenting here.

3: The third purpose is to make available here the most esoteric text from Rudolf Steiner, outside of the First Class, concerning the forming of the eternal ego or Higher-Self; this quest is referred to by Rudolf Steiner as "the most important life-question of all" ('Die allerwichtigste Frage" GA 138, 28th Aug. 1912). This is the theme of the First Class, but this other text, which I provide here in an Appendix, teaches us about this high spiritual task, from a very different, and very exalted perspective. It is equal in personal esoteric significance to Lesson 19.

4: Since we do not have the approximately 20 or so additional First Class Lessons that Rudolf Steiner had intended to give, it is my hope that this book presents the verses of the 19 Lessons that we do have, in an accurate and insightful form.

5: Rudolf Steiner has made it clear that the First Class may be considered to be part of an esoteric 'School' established by the great, majestic Archangel Michael several centuries ago, in spiritual realms, to provide spiritual direction and nurture for souls who would be living in modern times. It is my sincere hope that this book, in clarifying the meaning of the verses given in the First Class, will be of assistance to the "Michael School".

6: Finally, I am presenting here for the first time, images of the Ahrimanic and the Luciferic Doubles, which Rudolf Steiner presented in a veiled way, so that they are only cognized by the periphery of our consciousness.

The scope and structure of this book

It is my hope to publish a full First Class book at some time in the future; that is, a book with all of the Class Lessons of Rudolf Steiner, in a new, corrected translation, incorporating my translations of the verses. Since most people who use the First Class verses will be familiar with the Lessons, but are using inaccurate translations of the verses themselves, it seems more helpful to release this book now, rather than delay publication of the corrected verses.

To facilitate the use of the verses, I have sought to fit each verse onto one page, with the original German facing the English version. This does mean that at times there will be a blank page before the verses belonging to the next Lesson are given.

Large fonts have been used for the verses on these pages, for a user-friendly effect.

A number of illustrations have been included, either from Rudolf Steiner or from classical artistic sources, which help the reader to enter into the message or mood of a verse.

INTRODUCTION

Historical background

As noted earlier, Rudolf Steiner had undertaken for ten years, a similar task to that of the First Class, from 1904 to 1914. As General Secretary of the Theosophical Society, he gave esoteric Lessons in the German Branch of the Society to its members. This was carried out ostensibly in the Esoteric School of the Theosophical Society, but actually he taught from his own initiatory insights rather than from esoteric doctrines of the theosophical Esoteric School, an institution which had originally been established by H.P. Blavatsky. However in 1924, when Rudolf Steiner inaugurated the new phase of an esoteric schooling, he provided different material to that given in the earlier School. This later esoteric wisdom focused more especially on the demands made on the consciousness of an acolyte who is seriously intending to develop an awareness of the spiritual worlds.

Only 19 Lessons had been offered, apart from seven 'Recapitulatory Lessons', before September 1924, at which time he became too ill to continue his work. These meditative lessons with their verses were kept private and confidential by the Anthroposophical Society, but in the 1970's the independent Steiner Archives published them, in a limited manner; this began a process of giving people wider access to them. Later, from about 2005, they became available to anyone via the Internet. These Lessons are naturally regarded as sacred, and originally only the mantric verses were made available as private material, for members of the General Anthroposophical Society. This had been an appropriate and valid attitude at that time, instituted by Rudolf Steiner himself. His intention was to provide a deep meditative link for the members of the Anthroposophical Society to the spiritual source of the anthroposophical wisdom; and this link would be undermined, he explained, if this privileged material was accessed by opponents or indifferent persons. Even the members could not access the commentary of Rudolf Steiner in each Lesson, until recent years. Prior to this, they could only receive a copy of the verses for each Lesson. The members were given to understand that to offer these verses to other people was unethical – and this attitude reflected Rudolf Steiner's earlier statements. But he later commented that the Lessons could be published if they were to fall into the hands of unauthorized people.

After his death, in March of 1925, their status as 'private material', and hence not available to other people, was maintained by the Anthroposophical Society right though to the 1990's. But in fact already in 1924 and then the 1930's these texts were improperly made available to people who were either antagonistic to anthroposophical wisdom or indifferent to it.[2] The fact of the widespread availability of the texts for many years was not disclosed to the members for decades; this was a social situation which became irrelevant with the publication of the Lessons on the internet.[3]

The underlying dynamic – the Divine enchanted within the Cosmic Cross

The verses take the meditant through a process, focussing on quite specific aspects of the development of higher consciousness. There is a dynamic which these Lessons are offering. They are to assist the meditant to awaken the enchanted Divine from its slumber on her or his own 'cross' or fourfold earthly nature. That is, the verses seek to help the meditant to start to sense, and perhaps even experience, the actual spiritual realities existing within the soul, behind the everyday features of the human personality

---

[2] A cult figure on the edge of the Anthroposophical Society gave this material to some vehement opponents of anthroposophy, in the 1930's. Also, in the 1960's a leader of a splinter group of anthroposophists made them available to many people.
[3] Although this link has been broken by such actions, I believe this does not dissipate their power to assist individual meditants to achieve profound spiritual states.

or earthly self. In other words, the verses are a means by which the meditant may become aware of the spiritual powers and cosmic forces within feeling, thinking and will.

It is very helpful to realize that many of the Class Lessons are therefore meditations upon a theme which, through Plato, has become well-known in spiritual and literary circles: the immersion of the 'World-Soul' upon the fourfold cross of matter; or the spirit enchanted in the Cosmic Cross. The expression, 'World-Soul' is better expressed through anthroposophical wisdom as 'Soul of the Cosmos', meaning the divine Logos, whose influence, through the various hierarchies, underlies the cosmos. But there is an esoteric Christian aspect to this theme, as Rudolf Steiner explained in 1902:

> In the cross of Golgotha we have the same concept as we have in the philosophy of Plato, in which the All-Spirit {*the Soul of the World*} is crucified {*in the fourfold material world.*}[4]

As I wrote in *Rudolf Steiner's esoteric Christianity in the Grail painting by Anna May*, the statement from Plato about the World-soul (in his *Timaeus,* Sections 33 & 34) is somewhat complex, as the Greek text is ambiguous in places and quite abrupt. Plato is explaining here the spatial and geometrical aspects of how Creation came about. It is in the process of this, that he presents the profoundly potent idea of the Divine Spirit existing within, or rather, discreetly behind, the physical universe (probably in effect, the solar system). This Cosmos-Spirit or 'Soul of the Cosmos', is put there by the First Deity (the Father-God, in Christian terms). Plato begins section 34 saying,

> Such was the over-all plan of the eternal God {*'Reason-endowed Deity'*}, about the God then coming-into-being {*'reasoning Deity'*}; {*for whom he made*} a smooth and even body, having a surface in every direction.....and in the centre {*the Sun*} he put Soul and spread this out throughout the entirety {*of creation*}... (trans. the author)

To the ancient Greeks, divine beings, as distinct from nature spirits and other similar entities, were endowed with spiritual consciousness or high cosmic intelligence; they used the word 'reason' for such divine beings. Here Plato is teaching that the second deity (the Logos) would also manifest such cosmic intelligence, but not to such a degree as the Father-God; however, its powers of consciousness would increase with time.[5] Although Plato's language is obscure, one sees the idea being presented here is that, implicit within the physical world, interwoven in the different nature realms, is the Divine: an idea which is defined as 'panentheism'.

Although Plato does not state it directly, the implication is also that eventually, from the secondary deity, (the Soul of the Cosmos), humanity will emerge. So within humanity, 'behind' the earthly personality, the divine qualities of this great Soul of the Cosmos exist, as if slumbering. This teaching is echoed in the concept found in the Prologue to St. John's Gospel, of the 'Logos' who derives from the Father-God, and from whom all things in turn have been created; in particular, humanity. So, within the human being, the Divine or the 'Logos' is slumbering; or in other words, the threefold soul has a potential to develop a threefold spiritual capacity. In addition, in a later paragraph, Plato refers to Creation as having an 'X' shape, or fourfold shape which is a cross shape, although on an angle. So the Divine is held in, or 'imprisoned' in, the fourfold World Cross.

Very early Christian writers, perceiving this Idea, saw a resonance between their religion, wherein Jesus was crucified on a cross and Plato's very influential idea, by pointing out that Plato had taught that the divine Soul of the World was 'crucified' on a (world-)cross.[6] Rudolf Steiner agreed with this conclusion, and gave a deeper understanding of this by

---

[4] Archive lecture, 1st Mar.1902, Berlin.
[5] This subtle distinction between the two deities is expressed by Plato using a word for this second being which is a passive participle (logistheis, λογισθεὶς), rather than the noun, 'reason' (logismos, λογισμός) In Plato's Greek: Οὗτος δὴ πᾶς ὄντος ἀεὶ λογισμος Θεου περὶ τὸν ποτὲ ἐσόμενον Θεον λογισθεὶς λειον...
[6] Justin Martyr, in *Apol. 1*, para. 60 and Irenaeus of Lyons in, *The Proof of Apostolic Preaching.*

explaining that the concept behind Plato's words leads to a profound realization of the four realms of existence: mineral, plant, animal and human, as graded manifestations of 'God', that is, of divine beings as they manifest the creative intentions of the Logos, who is the vessel of the Father-god. In other words, the Divine is present, in an obscured state in the mineral realm, but stirs in the plants, arises to a dream-like state in the astral dynamics of the animals and awakens in humanity, with its sense of self: especially when the human being develops the 'Spiritual-self' (also called 'Spirit-self').

Rudolf Steiner explains that when Jesus was placed on the cross, then – in an awe-inspiring echo of the esoteric truth preserved by Plato – the Divine was stretched out on, or caught by, the fourfold material world.[7] So, in the Class Lessons, it is as if each meditant has to realize that the human being, with its threefold soul, is stretched out, or immersed within, the fourfold cross of the material world; a world which has three cardinal dynamics: from above, from the horizontal plane and from below.

The influences from 'Above' are from the zodiac, (these affect our thinking); the influences from 'Below' are from the subterranean depths (and affect our will), and from the 'Horizon', meaning in effect, the rising and setting planets, (these effect our feelings). All of this occurs within the fourfold environs of mineral, plant, animal and human life-waves; and these are sustained by the four ethers, together with the elemental beings within these.

But the intention of the gods in creating humanity, and in placing human beings with a threefold soul within the fourfold physical world, is that the higher triad of our spirit, the Spirit-self, Life-spirit and Spirit-human, can be brought into being, through many incarnations in this environment. This threefold reality is our eternal Higher-self or the slumbering Logos. **In the First Class, many Lessons are in effect pathways towards awakening our Divine potential, immersed in the Cosmic Cross.** The higher spiritual aspect of the meditant exists in the cosmos, without this actually being realized by most human beings. The verses are ways to help the meditant cognize their greater macrocosmic potential slumbering within their everyday astrality.

An overview of the underlying dynamic which the meditant is guided through, in the Class Lessons and their associated verses.

Lesson 1 & 2: the Double
The first two Lessons bring the meditant to awareness of their Lower-self or so-called 'Double'; and how these must be cognized and gradually overcome if he or she is to 'cross the Threshold', that is, to develop a higher consciousness or clairvoyance. (Without awareness of the very real Lower-self, New Age movements so easily lead their followers into a subtly enhanced egotism, or to an alienation from the Earth.)

Lesson 3: the Divine enchanted in the Cosmic Cross
A gentle focus on gaining awareness of the cosmic energies which form a counterpart to our soul-life.

Lesson 4: the Divine enchanted in the Cosmic Cross
A more direct awareness of the cosmic energies forming a counterpart to our soul-life.

Lesson 5: the Double as a debased spirit-reality lurking in the fourfold Cosmic Cross
Guidance concerning the Luciferic and Ahrimanic forces in the soul-life.

---

[7] Lecture, 29th May 1905 (GA 93), and in his *Christianity as Mystical Fact*.

Lesson 6: the Double in the etheric body
Insights into the Luciferic and Ahrimanic forces in the etheric-body

Lesson 7: the Divine enchanted in the Cosmic Cross
A more direct contemplation of the cosmic energies forming a counterpart to our soul-life.

Lesson 8: the cosmic matrix of our soul-forces as a mirror-image of these forces
A contemplation of the cosmic energies active in our soul-life, and how these interweave between each other.

Lesson 9: twofold – the elementals and our etheric body, and merging our threefold astrality
Meditative guidance about the Luciferic and Ahrimanic forces in the etheric-body.

Note: Lesson 10 is actually threefold:
10a: the zodiac and humanity
   contemplating the influence of the zodiac on humanity

10b: the pre-conception phase of our existence
   an exercise for awakening awareness of our existence prior to conception

10c: the past life
   an exercise for awakening awareness of one's existence in the past life

11: a powerful Cosmic Cross meditation to assist the acolyte to query what is the "I"
A profound meditation to awaken the Divine, the eternal Spirit-self, slumbering within the soul.

12: the Divine in the planetary spheres – the Hierarchies in our thinking and feeling
A meditation which guides one through the planetary spheres to an awakening of the Divine within the soul.

13: the Divine in the planetary spheres – the Hierarchies in our willing
A continuation of lesson 12.

14: the etheric body between Lucifer, Christ and Ahriman
Guidance regarding overcoming the debased elemental influences in the four ethers.

15: guidance about transcending the ethers' influence through the Hierarchies' influence
A dialogue of the Hierarchies about three of the ethers in our etheric body.

16: the fourth ether in the etheric body: the Cosmic Cross and the Hierarchies
A continuation of lesson 15: the fourth ether and then awakening the Divine in the Cosmic Cross.

17: the rainbow as a portal to the Hierarchies
The interaction of the Hierarchies with soul-life of human beings.

18: the Hierarchies and the threefold soul
The interaction of the Hierarchies with soul-life of human beings.

19: the first intimations of the eternalized 'I'
The awakening of the Divine within the Cosmic Cross, but now within the higher 'I' of the meditant.

****

The Prelude Verse

The verses of each lesson can be thought of as commencing with a 'Prelude Verse', because after the first few lessons, Rudolf Steiner started to use a specific verse, which could be called 'the Prelude Verse', before each lesson. This verse helps the meditant enter the mood necessary for working with a particular lesson. As Rudolf Steiner points out in his book, *Knowledge of Higher Worlds*, the meditative work only succeeds if the soil has entered into the mood of holiness, or reverence, prior to contemplating the meditative verse.

Actually, this Prelude verse was not created especially for the First Class. It was given about a year before to a small group of young people, who had asked Rudolf Steiner for assistance with their inner work, prior to the First Class's inauguration.[8]

This verse is given in German and in my translation, over the page. The small numbers on the edge of the page refer to the Notes which are found on the page following the English version.

---

[8] These people soon formed the "Youth Circle", and in the course of years, as they aged beyond the mid-thirties, the group was renamed, the "Michael Circle".

Prelude Verse in German

O Mensch, erkenne dich selbst !

So tönt das Weltenwort.

Du hörst es seelenkräftig

Du fühlst es geistgewaltig.

Wer spricht so weltenmächtig ?

Wer spricht so herzinniglich ?

Wirkt es durch des Raumes Weitenstrahlung

in deines Sinnes Seinserleben ?

Tönt es durch der Zeiten Wellenweben

In deines Lebens Werdestrom ?

Bist du es selbst, der sich

Im Raumesfühlen, im Zeiterleben

Das Wort erschafft, dich fremd

Erfuhlend in Raumes Seelenleere,

Weil du des Denkens Kraft

Verlierst im Zeitvernichtungsstrome ?

The Prelude Verse

O human being, cognize yourself !   1

Thus sounds the Cosmic Word.   2

You hear it powerfully with your soul,

You feel it mightily with your spirit.

Who is speaking with such cosmic might ?

Who is speaking with such intimacy to the heart ?

Is it efficacious in your senses' experience of being

from the bright, wide expanses of space ?

Does it resound in your life's stream of becoming

from the cyclical waves of time ?   3

Is it you, yourself, who –

in the sensing of space,

in the experiencing of time,

are creating this Word;

feeling dimly within estranged

in space's soul-emptiness,   4

because you are losing

the capacity for higher awareness   5

in the annihilating flow of time ?

COMMENTARY ON THE PRELUDE VERSE

1 "cognize yourself": is usually rendered, "know yourself". But the correct full meaning is, '**cognitively** know yourself', or briefly expressed, 'cognize yourself'. This is not simply "know yourself" in the sense of self-reflection based on rational analysis of one's given personality. For the verb used here has three meanings, or rather three nuances of the one meaning, namely: to cognize, to know, and to realize. So the verse is saying, strive to perceive (with your consciousness) your actual higher, truer Self, and thereby come to know what this Self is. Such striving of one's consciousness to directly cognize spiritual realities, and to thus transcend matter, is the essential key to crossing the threshold. In future occurrences of this phrase, I shall generally use, "know yourself".

2 "the cosmic Word": the German term *Wort* appears here, as 'Word', but this singular term can also be rendered in the plural, 'words' (hence a saying, or a maxim, or an adage). However, it also can mean something entirely **non-verbal**. We say of many things that they 'speak' to us; e.g., the architecture of a room, or the shape of a plant or animal. Rudolf Steiner specifically states that this term, 'Word' in this context is just a stand-in or surrogate for a longer phrase.[9] It is an abbreviation for something like, 'the palpable impact upon us, in some intangible, subtle way, of some part of creation, resounding to us as a kind of soundless word'. It is a mistake to think of the 'cosmic Word' as an articulated speaking to us by the cosmos; in fact a very modern term, 'signifier', is actually an accurate way to translate this German phrase. So the term, 'cosmic signifier' is just as useful here.

3 "The cyclical waves of time": the German text could literally mean, 'in time's weaving of waves' (the usual translation), but here it is more likely to mean: 'time's bringing-forth of undulations {or waves}'. The German word 'weben' often does not mean 'weaving', but 'a tracing out', or 'a bringing forth'. Furthermore in his preliminary version of this verse, Rudolf Steiner wrote: "in the cycles of time". So, I have here combined both phrases.

4 The unusual term, '**space's soul-emptiness**' is a contracted way of saying, 'space as something devoid of any soul content', which is the actual meaning of the German phrase. The implication is that space is perceived as empty by modern humanity, as devoid of any living, astral qualities; space is a void in regard to any subtle ambiences.

5 The term '**higher awareness**' is much more correct than the usual translation 'thinking', as the meaning here is not modern logical thought, which is what we all mean today by the word 'thinking' or 'thought'. Here the term 'thinking' means the holistic insights, the semi-psychic consciousness naturally possessed by people in earlier ages (as referred to in Lesson Two). We need to be aware that to Rudolf Steiner, the term 'thinking' was not restricted to what we today mean by 'thinking'. To him, it also meant any of the three higher clairvoyant consciousness states, called 'pure thought' or 'non-sensory thought'.
For example,
".. *in diesem reinen Denken wird man herausgehoben aus dem Leib in eine Welt, die nicht irdische ist...*" = "in this pure thinking one is led up out of the body into a world which is not earthly." (GA 257 p.54)

Or,"..*dann kommt der Mensch endlich dazu....ein Bilderbewußtsein zu entwickeln, in Bildern nicht träumen, sondern denken zu können.*" = then the human being finally develops a (psychic) image consciousness, not dreaming in images, but thinking in (astral) images. (GA 79 p.48)
The theme of losing the capacity for holistic-psychic higher awareness, which especially appeared as from the year 333 AD, is taught specifically in a later Class Lesson, and in various Members' lectures.

---

[9] *Man in the Light of Occultism, Theosophy and Philosophy*, GA 137, lecture 12.

A Guardian Verse

There is also another verse, which was given about six months before the First Class was founded, which is also helpful as a Prelude Verse. It was introduced by Rudolf Steiner in the 18th Class lesson.

The German Original

Erkenne erst den ernsten Hüter,

Der vor des Geisterlandes Pforten steht,

Den Einlaß deiner Sinnenkraft

Und deines Verstandes Macht verwehrend,

Weil du in Sinnesweben

Und im Gedankenbilden

Aus Raumeswesenlosigkeit,

Aus Zeiten Truggewalten

Des eignen Wesens Wahrheit

Dir kraftvoll erst erobern mußt.

First, cognize the earnest Guardian

who is placed before the threshold of

Spiritland, barring entrance to your senses' capacity

and to your power of intelligence, because

you must first powerfully attain through effort –

in what the senses display before us,

and in forming of mental images,

from the non-substantiality of space,

and from time's deceptive might –

the truth of your own being !

1

Notes to the earlier 'Guardian verse':

1 "...**must first powerfully attain through effort**": 'attain' instead of "conquer". This is a better rendering than suggesting the need to 'conquer knowledge' of the truth of one's own being, for the acolyte has to **attain** to her or his true self, not lay siege to it and conquer it. The German verb 'erobern' used here, can also mean, apart from 'conquer', to 'attain through effort'. The great German writer Herder, for example used it in this way, speaking of the efforts by scholars to translate Babylonian texts, in the 19th century,

> "…..da es jetzt von allen Seiten so stark auf die Keil- oder Pfeilschrift losgehet um ihre kenntnis zu erobern.

> = "…..da es jetzt von allen Seiten so stark auf die Keil- oder Pfeilschrift losgehet um ihre kenntnis zu erobern.

> = This means, in English;

"for everywhere one is now really focused on the arrow-headed or cuneiform language (of Mesopotamia) in order to attain knowledge of it {through such effort}."

Correcting translations of the initial verse for Lesson One

It is right at the beginning of this first Lesson that we encounter the many major changes needed in the translations of its verses, as published for use in the Anthroposophical Society. Consequently, as from this first Lesson, the reader will encounter substantial differences in the translations provided here. Apart from providing a correction of various errors in the commonly used translations, another reason for the new translations is to reveal a previously unknown meaning, concealed within the ambiguous German words in some of the verses. To indicate the basis of my statement that there are major errors in the understanding of many of these Verses, we shall explore the result of my work, (both meditative and scholarly work), concerning Lesson One. This will help to explain why there are, in other places in the 19 verses, some quite significant differences between my translations and those that have been used for many decades.

For Lesson One, we only need at first to consider now in detail the first ten lines of the Verse. This verse conveys, says Rudolf Steiner, the words spoken to the meditant by the Guardian of the Threshold.

In the commonly used versions, these lines read like this:

> Where on earthly foundations, colour upon colour,
> the Life-creative manifests itself,   (or, life creatively manifests itself)
> Where from earthly substances, form on form,
> lifeless substance shapes itself,
> Where sentient beings, powerful in will,
> warm themselves happily through their own existence,
> Where you, O Man, gain your bodily existence
> from earth and air and light.
>
> There you enter your own true being's
> cold, night-enveloped darknesses........

But this, and all similar versions contain substantial errors, and only present the first, the less esoteric, meanings. To unveil the deeper meaning, we need to start with the very first phrase of line one, which, in the commonly used versions, is rendered as 'earthly foundations' (or 'earthly grounds'). The term in German is 'Erdengründen'. It is possible to translate this word as 'earthly foundations', but this German phrase usually has other meanings. For example,

1: reasons / logical bases / causes   (when used in philosophy and logic)
2: the Earth's depths / interior   (but only if speaker is **on** the Earth)
3: the Earth's topsoil, in which the plants grow, on which people and animals walk
4: Earth's foundations (the soil and rock layers, with its chemicals, etheric forces, etc.)

The common versions, with this interpretation, 'earth foundations', then go on to say:

Version A: "life manifests": or something called "Life-creative" manifests, and in so doing, is creating the world. This creating is made obvious via various coloured objects.

Version B: "life manifests creatively"; again this is made obvious via various coloured objects.

We notice how the phrase 'colour upon colour' is floating rather loosely around in both of these versions, and the reader has to add the word "in" to make sense of the line:

"the Life-creative manifests itself, (or, life creatively manifests itself) in colour upon colour."

In his commentary, Rudolf Steiner points out with regard to these lines, that nature is creative, and a magnificent world of nature, of many coloured and shaped objects, lies all around us. Consequently, this is how the beginning of the verse has been understood. But we shall soon see that this is only the surface meaning; for the German text discreetly has another, quite different, meaning placed in it. And this much deeper meaning was in fact indicated by Rudolf Steiner himself. But for now let's pass on to the next couplet, in the usual versions:

> Where from earthly substances, form on form,
> lifeless substance shapes itself,

Here we learn that the mineral realm, or inanimate matter, somehow shapes itself. We shall soon see that this is not catching the full subtle meaning of the German text. Then the next couplet in the common translations says,

> Where sentient beings, powerful in will,
> warm themselves with joy through their own existence

We shall soon see that this translation is seriously in error. These lines appear to affirm the commentary of Rudolf Steiner, namely that the animals, frolicking and moving about, are experiencing pleasure in their simple existence, and that they are determined to do this. However, once again, it will become obvious that there is actually a much much deeper meaning to this couplet (and to the earlier couplets) once it is correctly understood. However before we reconsider these first six lines, to discover their deeper meaning, one needs to consider, in a correct translation, the following, rather startling lines which come soon after these six lines:

> There you enter your own being's
> cold, night-enveloped darknesses........

Whereas the usual translations incorrectly have:

> There you enter your own **true** being's
> cold, night-enveloped darknesses........

There is here a startling misunderstanding which the next lines reveal.
For the above couplet is followed by these words:

> For your own being, day darkens to
> soul-night, to spiritual dimness

And at this point, with these latest lines, if we are alert and using the above corrected version, we see how we are being given here the solemn message that our incarnate, earthly state of consciousness is actually a condition of inner coldness and spiritual darkness. Then we begin to realize that there has to be another veiled message in the first lines; for the message in these later lines contradicts the feeling, the general impression, that the six first lines give us, in the common translations, since these emphasize the magnificence of nature.

Now, it is quite true that the impression arising from the usual translations does harmonize with most of Rudolf Steiner's commentary – but the perceptive reader discovers that in his commentary, Rudolf Steiner also **briefly points to another, very different, message**. A message which is fully in harmony with the message about "inner coldness and spiritual darknesses". Let's see now these first six lines in a much more esoterically-informed translation, which reveals the deeper initiation messages.

There is here not only the simple message,

> Where on earthly foundations, colour upon colour,
> the Life-creative manifests itself,

because, the same German words are also saying, on a deeper level,

> Where in spirit-distant earthly places,
> colour upon colour manifests,
> calling forth existence;

This is because the German phrase usually rendered as 'earthly foundations' also has another meaning, namely a meaning of high importance for spiritual literature:

"earthly places, distant from spirit realms (especially Devachan)".

This German phrase in classical literature is used to mean a place far away from where you are, or where the speaker is located. So in fairy tales, one reads of a little hut "in Waldesgründen", which means, 'deep in the interior of the forest'. This is actually the deeper meaning of the phrase in this Class verse. It is this same meaning which is used in a poetic or esoteric sense by great German writers **including Rudolf Steiner himself**. In a spiritual text, it means earthly places which are far removed from 'the heavenly heights', or Devachan. This is obviously a far more profound meaning than 'earthly (chemical) foundations/or the topsoil'.

For example:
From Richard Wagner (in his opera, Tannhaüser)
> O du, hoch über diesen **Erdengründen**, die mir den Engel meines Heil's gesandt: erbarm' dich mein, der ach ! so tief in Sünden, schmachvoll des Himmelsmittlerin verkannt.

> O thou, high above these earthly places, remote from spirit realms, who sent to me the Angel, for my well-being – have pity upon me, who is, oh ! so deep in sins.......

Not:
O thou, high above these *earthly chemical foundations*, who sent to me the Angel for my well-being....

From **the opera by Dvorak, Die heilige Ludmila**

> *Chor Der Engel*
> Aus hohem Reich umstrahlt von Morgenrot,
> neigt euch hinab zu tiefen **Erdengründen**,
> sein Antlitz will der Herr dem Lande zeigen,
> laßt seine Taube aufs Land niedersteigen.

> *Choir of the Angels*
> From a lofty realm, enveloped by morning dawn,
> descend ye down **to earthly-places far distant from the spirit**,
> for the Lord God wills to reveal his countenance,
> letting his dove descend to the ground.

Not:
.....descend ye down to *deep foundations of earthly soil and rocks....*

FROM RUDOLF STEINER
(In book number 40A - *Sprüche Dichtungen Mantren – Ergänzungsband,* p. 50)

> Ihr, die aus Geistes Helle niedersteigt ins Erdendunkel,
> um in Daseins Widerstreben Geistesleuchten zu entfalten,
> Geisteswärme zu entflammen, Geisteskräfte zu erwirken.
> Euch durchwärme meine Liebe,
> leuchtend Denken, ruhend Fühlen, heilend Wollen,
> Daß, in Geisteshöhen wurzelnd,
> **In den Erdengründen** wirkend,
> Ihr des Wortes Diener werdet Geist erhellend.

> In English:

> Ye, who descend down from spirit brightness
> into earthly darkness, in order
> - in existence's counter-striving –
> to unfold spiritual radiance,
> to enflame spiritual warmth,
> to make efficacious spiritual energies –
> en-warm ye my love:
> radiant thinking, tranquil feeling, healing Will,
> so that ye – originating in spiritual heights –
> may become servants of the Word,
> efficacious in **spirit-distant earthly places.**
> (Or: in **earth's realm, spiritland distant.**) [10]

Not: "efficacious in the molecular substances and life-forces of the soil".

So the first line in the verse of Lesson One is – "Where in spirit-distant earthly places" – for this is its real, deeper meaning; a meaning emphasizing an important point **from the perspective of the Guardian.** He exists in a high and remote spiritual realm: in the sun-sphere, at the entry to Devachan. We need to note that this Devachanic state or consciousness **is precisely what the initiation path seeks to offer to the acolyte.** The Guardian is contrasting the sensory awareness, far away, down in the Earth realm, with that of Devachan, in an admonishing way.

Secondly, we also now have,

> colour upon colour manifests,   (Wo auf Erdengründen, Farb' an Farbe,)
> calling forth existence;   (Sich das Leben schaffend offenbart)

It has not been realized that the singular verb here, 'manifests', can be related to the many colours, because each of the manifold colours is actually a separate, single colour; single objects, which match the singular verb. This second meaning becomes disclosed once we realize that this is the case. The esoterically insightful person now realizes two things: firstly, that the surface meaning here, about nature being creative, as given in the usual versions, is the surface meaning. It is a gentle introduction, and is self-evident to any person, for one does not need the Guardian to reveal that nature is creative.

But the message about our earthly nature, perceiving the colours of the physical environs, through the sense of sight, which results in physical existence being conjured up (as a full and convincing reality), by the sheer predominance of our visual sense, is not a mundane statement. It is about what in the Indian world is called 'Maya'. This deeper meaning was never seen, despite Rudolf Steiner himself indicating it in his commentary, "*...we have derived our physical body from out of all that which forms around us - that* *which is 'greening and growing' in colour upon colour.*" The two German verbs used here (in English, as the participles 'greening' and 'growing') are both in the singular, because each of the many colours are, in themselves, singular. Let's note here, that in earlier Ages, a more pictorial approach was used for acolytes entering the Mysteries; strange images were carved on the walls of the ante-chamber of ancient Mystery temples. These images put this question to the acolyte: are you actually wanting to enter into a consciousness state or spiritual realm, where such strange beings (or un-earthly dynamics) are everywhere experienced ? If so, you shall need a different, a higher, power of perceiving to do this. Can you meet the challenges involved in this quest?

But now, in the new Christ-centred Mysteries, the acolyte is taught that their sensory perceptions and consequently their thinking too, is matter-bound, and this is due to the power of the physical senses, especially that of sight. Our 'maya' consciousness, which regards the mineral-physical realm as reality, is due to the predominance of the visual sense, the seeing of the physical world around us, that is, objects with their colours. The deeper meaning of these lines then, is about the prevailing earth-bound state of the mind today, and how this is due to the power of the physical sensing. It is telling us that our consciousness is bound to the physical world, with its many coloured objects, which our eyes so directly perceive. It is just this perception, which we, since our infancy have been subjected to, which the initiatory path seeks to overcome.

In other words, it is this perceiving, by its colours, of the sense world, through our eyes, which conjures up existence or earthly life before us, in a very convincing way. The verb used here 'schaffen' (to create), can also be used in this more poetic way, referring to the calling forth or conjuring up of something; it does not have to mean literally 'creating'. This sensory 'illusion' produced by our visual sensing is emphasized in the great artwork of the large cupola of the Goetheanum, where, as the next step after the creation of the world by the Elohim, two large eyes (and ears) are portrayed. It is the effect of Ahriman's activity, that in sensing and seeing the physical world, human beings find themselves within a physical realm, and are soon convinced that this is the only reality.

It is important to note here, that Rudolf Steiner himself indicated this second, deeper meaning, briefly, **in his own commentary**. To really grasp this, we need to recall the lines further on, where we are told that in the physical world we encounter our own cold, deep spiritual darkness. In his commentary about Lesson One, Rudolf Steiner comments that, that, "*....in all the beauty, in all the greatness, in all the grandeur, of Nature, **there is present a spiritual darkness***". This short statement has been not fully appreciated, and hence only the surface meaning of these verses has ever been known. But it is this dominance of physical cognizing, down in earthly places, and its influence on our consciousness, which is being contrasted here, on the deeper level of the German text, to the sublime sense-free cognition, far away in Devachan.

Actually, the first six lines of Verse One point to, in sequence, the physical, the etheric and the astral realities, but in a way deeply relevant to the enigma of human consciousness. The first two lines alert the acolyte to the fact that they are tapping on a door which, if opened, demands that their consciousness be prepared to rise above the 'Maya' sense-bound state. Then having firstly referred to the seeing of the mineral-physical world as 'existence' (but indicating it is an illusion), the verse goes on, in the next two lines, to point to the activity of the ethers, indicating that through them, matter is mysteriously shaped and given texture,

> Where, from earthly matter,
> form upon form gives shape and texture
> to the Inanimate;

Here we see that earthly matter does not just form itself, as in the usual translations, but rather that the many separate forms are giving shape and texture to matter; and this points to the effectiveness of the ethers from within these forms. Then in the third set of lines **the focus is the astral reality**; however, the deeper meaning of these two lines has not been seen, hence the common translations have never reflected the meaning of these lines. The usual versions have:

> Where sentient beings, powerful in will,
> warm themselves with joy in their existence

But the correct translation is:

> Where resolutely, Beings, with dim inner-awareness,
> by their own existence, happily warm themselves;

The errors in the common versions include firstly, not comprehending the meaning of a very rare verb, 'erfühlen'. The normal translations have, 'sentient being', which is incorrect. The verb 'erfühlen' used here is extremely rare, and does **not** mean simply 'sentient' or, 'to feel'. It means a sentient awareness **which is inwardly dim or subdued**, i.e., a vague inner sensing. This rare verb was no longer noted, even in huge dictionaries, already by 1900. It was frequently used in the 17th to 19th centuries, and it was very often used by Rudolf Steiner: some 600 times in his recorded 4,200 lectures. To work with this verse it is obviously necessary to understand this verb.[11]

In his commentary, Rudolf Steiner briefly refers to animals moving around, enjoying their existence; and so the common translations, giving the surface meaning of this third couplet, can appear to be confirmed by his own words. But seen more clearly, it becomes obvious that the acolyte, in being given by a Hierophant an initial over-view of material existence, and a hint of the etheric forces being active in matter, now has another, very important task of self-knowledge. The acolyte should start to perceive that, in the complex tapestry of, not only animals, but also normal human beings, **there is truly an unquestioning, hence indistinct or semi-conscious awareness of their own inner self or nature. And there is especially a lack of interest in the core theme of the initiatory quest: the eternal Higher-self.** The lack of any real awareness of one's ego – as a potential higher ego – is being pointed out here.

Secondly, the phrase, 'strong of will', in the common versions, is not accurate here. The German phrase used can certainly mean this, but it can also mean 'determinedly' or 'resolutely' – in the sense of strong **astral** urges, and **not** a strong will, in the higher, true sense. To see the initiatory meaning here, we need to understand that human beings have two kinds of 'will'. One is the 'Will' proper: that mysterious, subconscious soul power which can arise with extraordinary speed and strength when we are in an emergency situation, and which is the major force behind the digestive and the immune systems.

Whereas the other 'will' is really only determined urges, stemming from strong desires or yearnings; these are quite accessible to our conscious mind. But the real Will is not derived from earthly desires; it is a higher force in the astral body, and is mainly subconscious, although it can be awakened, ennobled and assimilated into the ego-sense, once it has been empowered by spiritual development.

It is directly from this dimmed state of awareness, in terms of the Higher-self, that the enjoyment of illusory pleasures, (and defending false values and hollow life-priorities) derive. It is precisely this semi-conscious cognizing of the self which has to be replaced by a vitally alert and questioning soul-state, and then later by a direct cognizing of the Higher-self. Unawakened people, and also animals, who with inner dimness of soul, enjoy the unquestioned, non-critiqued pleasures of their bodily nature – the subject of this line – can not possibly have a 'strong will' in the higher, true sense.

---

[11] I submitted my analyses of difficult phrases to a German Professor of Literature for his assessment. He has confirmed that all my interpretations are fully grammatically valid. I am also a Government accredited NAATI German -> English translator, and a translator of published academic material.

But they do have a resolute astrality, or astral 'will'. Strong astral determination can impel a person to become rich quite early in life, for example, but such a person may not be able to carry out the first of the six Basic Exercises which require a person to focus their thoughts on a very plain object for five minutes, day after day, for months. Nor would a person who has only strong astral determination (astral 'will') carry out the 'will exercise', the second of these six exercises. This involves performing a non-useful deed at a time, pre-determined some hours before; for this, the real, deeper Will is needed.

So on the deeper level, when the German is correctly translated, the verse here is highlighting the inner blindness of beings incarnate in matter, **including the acolyte**. The acolyte can still have a strong drive to enjoy the illusory pleasures that the physical world offers to a self-centred, un-enlightened soul state. People (and animals) whose astrality is immersed in matter are strongly determined to enjoy various illusory earthly pleasures. But the Guardian in speaking here, is pointing out how unsatisfactory and how unfree such a state really is. Before we go further with the verses and commentary of the Lessons, let's sum up what has been pointed out in regard to just the first lines of Verse One. The less esoteric meaning communicated here is,

> "Where on earth foundations, [in] colour upon colour,
> life creatively manifests"

This is simply a comment on the **capacity** of life to be creative, and the main evidence for this are the colours around us. And for the beginner in the spiritual path, it is of course valid to point this out. The same is true of the other version:

> "Where on earth foundations, [in] colour upon colour,
> life, creative, manifests"   (or, Life-Creative manifests)

But on the deeper, veiled, level, the Guardian is saying:

> "Where in spirit-distant earthly places,
> colour upon colour manifests,
> calling forth existence...."

The lesson here is that, down here on Earth, far away from Devachan, the visual sense conjures forth images to us, resulting in the ahrimanic illusion of creation or earthly existence as consisting of just the physical world. This deeper layer of meaning about our visual sense confronting the world of matter through its colours. This is subtly indicated by Rudolf Steiner himself in his commentary on this verse, "...*very rich glow of manifestations wells forth from everything around us...which sends colour into our eyes...*" And regarding the next two lines, not:

> Where from earthly matter, [in] form upon form,
> the lifeless substance takes on its shape,

This is only saying that the mineral realm becomes structured (from its own dynamics). Nor is it saying,

> Where from earthly matter, [in] form upon form,
> the lifeless substance takes on its [final] shape,

For this is saying only that the mineral realm becomes structured, somehow. But rather, the complex German text has the meaning:

> Where, from earthly matter,
> form upon form gives shape and texture
> to the Inanimate"

The deeper meaning here is an indication that etheric forces, manifesting through manifold shapes, are acting upon matter, bringing about the multitude of different shapes and textures. It also seems unlikely that this line is saying that the mineral realm takes up a final shape and stays that way, although the German verb does allow these meanings. It is more likely that this couplet is saying that the mineral realm, or inanimate matter, changes constantly, from one shape and texture into another; whether a grain of sand, the wing of a bird, the blossom of a flower, a plant leaf, etc. And in saying this, the attention of the acolyte is directed to the efficacy of the ether within the physical world. Also now, regarding the next two lines:
Not,

> Where sentient beings, powerful in will,
> warm themselves with joy in their existence

But rather, the German text is saying:

> Where resolutely, Beings, with dim inner-awareness,
> by their own existence, happily warm themselves;

So in these first six lines, on the deeper level, the Hierophant is viewing the facets of physical life, and astrality or sentiency, but precisely from the viewpoint of the soul who is beginning to seek enlightenment. This person must become aware that her or his assumptions are derived from sensory impressions, and that they have only a dim, earthly self-awareness and a naive enjoyment of material pleasures.

> Where, in spirit-distant earthly places,
> colour upon colour manifests,
> calling forth existence;
> Where, from earthly matter,
> form upon form gives shape and texture
> to the Inanimate;
> Where resolutely, Beings, with dim inner-awareness,
> by their own existence, happily warm themselves;

Once these first three sets of lines are understood on this deeper level, they also show an inner harmony in their structure, which reflects the German structure:

Where, in SPIRIT–DISTANT EARTHLY REALMS,
colour upon colour <u>manifests</u> calling forth *existence*;

Where, from EARTHLY MATTER,
form upon form <u>gives shape and texture</u> to *the inanimate* ;

Where resolutely, BEINGS WITH DIM INNER AWARENESS
by **their own existence** <u>happily</u> <u>warm</u> *themselves*

The next four lines are also in need of attention, for in the usual versions these are incorrectly rendered as this:

Where you, O human being, acquire your bodily existence　　(body/ bodily being)
from earth and air and light.
There you enter your own true being's
cold, night-enveloped darkness

But as we have already noted earlier, they are actually:

> Where you, O human being, acquire for yourself
> corporeal existence from earth and air and light.
> There you enter your own* being's　　　　　　　　(* separate)
> Deep, cold darkness, enveloped in night.

Here the emphasis is on a human being specifically acquiring corporeality (that is, bodily existence). This is a process which refers back to the earlier lines, pointing to the intention of the soul to become incarnate – precisely into "earthly places, distant from Spiritland", where matter-bound visual perceptions and earthly values predominate. This is why the German does **not** say, "acquire your bodily existence", but rather says, "acquire **for yourself** bodily existence". That is because then the Guardian, in communicating with the meditant, places emphasis on their deeper intentions and on the necessity by which one has to become incarnated into precisely this dark, illusion-bound, world of the flesh.

The next two lines in my translation differ even more widely from the common versions, which mistakenly refers to "entering your own **true** being's cold night-enveloped darkness...", whereas my translation follows Rudolf Steiner's words, and refers to entering "your **own** being's deep, cold darkness..." To insert the word "true" here is a very serious mistake. There is not a German word for "true" in this verse at all; a major misunderstanding, commencing decades ago and continuing on today, has led official translators to deliberately add this word. In this way, the meaning is destroyed, for these two lines are about the incarnate, Maya-bound, corporeal human being's earthly reality. And this is – when bluntly compared with the state of high spirituality that the initiation process offers – a *"deep, cold darkness, enveloped in night"*.

This is definitely not the state of the "true" spiritual nature of a person; for this does not possess an inner darkness and nowhere in this Class Lesson does Rudolf Steiner suggest that it does. He uses the German word 'eigen' here, which means 'own' in the sense of 'separate' – and this is exactly what the incarnate person becomes; a separated entity, encased in a body, no longer existing in a wonderfully light-filled, interconnected spiritual being-ness. Not to realize that these initial lines of the verse for Lesson One are about the illusory, earthly self, and its Doubles, means that **the core point being made** in the Lesson **has not been realized**. The Three Beasts, which are soon mentioned, are a more specific way of defining the earthly self's *"deep, cold darkness, enveloped in night"*.

The word "Eigenwesens" here means, one's own separate persona, separated from the spiritual worlds. But this same German word can also have a higher meaning, namely one's actual, specific self or individuated self – as something not lowly nor illusory. However, in this Introductory verse, it means simply the illusory, separated earthly personal self. But since the word does have two different meanings, to avoid confusion, Rudolf Steiner pointed out in regard to another verse which meaning is intended, (a verse for Lesson Three, in a Recapitulatory Lesson), which also includes this phrase. On that later occasion he told his audience, "**this time** it means 'selfhood' in **a good, higher sense**."[12] (emphasis mine, AA)

But despite this assistance from Rudolf Steiner, the word 'true' was inserted, because the message of the verse was not perceived, leading to confusion, already decades ago. This confusion was seemingly given confirmation when it was noted that in a different Lesson, (Recapitulatory Lesson no. 2, 9th Sept. 1924) Rudolf Steiner refers to "our soul-spiritual life, which is what exists before conception and birth: our own true human being-ness." But in this Lesson, this phrase occurs in a totally different context, where it refers to our human nature, prior to being drawn down into the body. [12]

Page 42, in vol.3 of the official German 'Erste Klasse' books; vol. 241c, 1977.

Whereas the similar phrase in this Introductory verse, "your own being's ..." is in fact referring to our incarnate illusory state, which has a "dark, cold night-enveloped" quality. But such a quality does not belong to the higher spiritual state; it does not have this, only the earthly state has a cold, night-enveloped state. So we cannot enter into our "own being's deep, cold darkness, enveloped in night", if we are referring to our higher soul-spiritual state, which we had when we were not yet incarnate beings. For this is a condition that we descend into, only by incarnating; by descending into the etheric-physical states of "earth, air and light".

So, to meditate on this phrase, "...your own true being's cold night-enveloped darkness..." is to be engaged an effort which cannot be successful as it has no meaning; and the same applies to the mistakes which we noted earlier. There are many more of these in the usual interpretation of the remaining 18 verses; these shall be clearly identified in the relevant sections of this book.

We have considered the first part of the verses in Lesson One, and seen why this book provides different translations to those normally used; at this point it will be helpful to include all of Lesson One, as given by Rudolf Steiner, incorporating these corrections to the verses, and finishing this Lesson with my translations of the verses, together with the German original, and my commentary (excepting for my commentary on the initial section of Verse One, which we have just explored).

Note: Omissions In presenting here the transcript of Lesson One given by Rudolf Steiner, any brief comments which deal with the internal affairs of the Anthroposophical Society, such as notice of change of dates for the next Lesson, etc, are omitted as these are no longer relevant.

It is my hope that all of the First Class Lessons of Rudolf Steiner, incorporating my new translations, can be made available in a new, larger book in the future. In the meantime, most people do have these Lessons, or can acquire them from the book market, so I am providing here accurate versions of the 19 verses and a commentary on them.

LESSON ONE by RUDOLF STEINER

My dear friends,

..... (omission of organizational remarks)

First of all, I would like to present to your hearts, and to your souls, what should be there, above our School, as a kind of engraved brass tablet. For it shall really be a matter of us fully identifying with what emerges from the life of the spirit into our soul's ear and our soul's understanding. In accordance with this, we shall begin with the words:
(Note: in providing here my translation here, I am both correcting the errors of the usual versions, and also giving the deeper, veiled meaning, rather than only the surface meaning.)

> Where in spirit-distant earthly places,
> colour upon colour manifests,
> calling forth existence;
> Where, from earthly matter,
> form upon form gives shape and texture
> to the Inanimate;
> Where resolutely, Beings with dim inner awareness
> by their own existence happily warm themselves;
> Where you, O human being, acquire for yourself
> corporeal existence, from earth and air and light:
>
> There you enter your own being's
> Deep, cold darkness, enveloped in night;
> You enquire never, in the dimness of space's wide expanse,
> Whom you are, and were, and shall become.
> For your own being, day darkens
> to soul-night, to spiritual dimness;
> and, in anxiety of soul, you turn towards the light
> which is empowered from out of the darknesses.

I will repeat it:

> Where in spirit-distant earthly places,
> colour upon colour manifests,
> calling forth existence;
> Where, from earthly matter,
> form upon form gives shape and texture
> to the Inanimate;
> Where resolutely, Beings with dim inner awareness
> by their own existence happily warm themselves;
> Where you, O human being, acquire for yourself
> corporeal existence, from earth and air and light:
>
> There you enter your own being's
> Deep, cold darkness, enveloped in night;
> You enquire never, in the dimness of space's wide expanse,
> Whom you are, and were, and shall become.
> For your own being, day darkens
> to soul-night, to spiritual dimness;
> and, in anxiety of soul, you turn towards the light
> which is empowered from out of the darknesses.

These words tell us that beautiful and glorious and great and lofty is the world, and that an endless glow of revelation wells forth to us in all that which emerges as living in the leaf and blossom, and which sends forth colour on colour to our eyes from the visible universe; it is meant to remind us how the divine is manifested in what is lifeless in earthly matter, in the thousands and many thousands of crystalline and non-crystalline forms beneath our feet, in the water and air, in clouds and stars. This should make clear to us that all this is divine-spiritual revelation: what as animal life frolics in the world delighting in its own existence, warms itself through its own existence. And this should also remind us that we derive our own bodies from all that which there is taking on form, and is greening and growing, in colour upon colour. But it should also make us aware that in all what is beautiful and lofty and splendid and divine to the senses, we ask in vain about what we ourselves are, as human beings.

Natural existence may shine towards us as grand and powerful, resounding in tone, encountering us with strength and raying-out warmth, but this can never give us information about ourselves, even though it does give us information about immense things, about a divine extensive reality, but it does not give us information about ourselves. For we always have to say to ourselves: that which we dimly sense as our inner self within, is not woven from what we encounter, as beauty and splendour and greatness and power of external nature, empowered from that part of nature which is not of humanity. And so the question arises for our soul: Why does that reality around about us, of which we are also a part, remain dark and silent?

And we must experience what we might feel as a kind of deprivation, to be actually a blessing. We need to experience it in this way: that we can say, in the deepest earnestness and clear sternness, 'We must first make ourselves truly human, into human beings who are warm in soul and strong of spirit, so that we may find, as Spirit in the human being, the Spirit in the world'. But for this it is necessary that we prepare ourselves, not in a light-hearted way, to come to the boundary of the sense-world, where the spirit's revelation can become perceptible to us. We must say to ourselves: if we were to arrive at this boundary unprepared, and the full light of the spirit and immediately comes upon us, then, because we have not yet developed the strength of spirit and the warmth of soul necessary for receiving the spirit, the spirit would shatter us, and cast us back into our nothingness.

It is for this reason that there exists at the boundary between the sense-world and spirit-world, that Herald of the gods, that Herald of the spirit, about whom we will hear more and more during the coming Lessons, whom we shall want to always know better and better. That Herald of the spirit is present there, who warningly speaks to us, telling us how we should be (as a spiritual person) and what we must lay aside, so that we may approach the revelations of the spiritual world in the right way.

And my dear friends, firstly we must understand, that with regard to all the beauty, greatness and the loftiness of nature, **there is present a spiritual darkness** at first, out of which the light must be born which tells us what we are and were and will be. Then we must realize that the first thing which must be understood, from out of the darkness, is that Spirit-herald, who is sending us the appropriate admonition. Therefore we let this Spirit-herald's words resound within our souls, and allow the description of this Spirit-herald to light up before our soul-eye.

> And out of the darknesses there brightens -
> revealing yourself in exact likeness

– the inner human being is addressed –

> yet also forming you into an allegory -
> an earnest spiritual signifier in the cosmic ether,
> audible to your heart, powerfully efficacious:

> The Herald of the Spirit - whom alone
> can illumine the path for you.

> In front of him, spreads out the fields of the senses,
> Behind him, there yawns the depths of the abyss.
> And before his darkened fields of the spirit
> at the edge of the yawning abyss of being
> there resounds his most powerful Creator-word:
> "Behold, I am the only portal to spiritual cognizing" !

We must be fully clear that we need to be aware of all that comes as warning from the Spirit-herald before we venture to fathom what is not found here on this side of the threshold, in the realm of the senses, instead on the other side of the yawning abyss, spreading out there spiritually. This is at first immersed in deep darkness, out of which, for human understanding, the only thing which lights up is that countenance of the Spirit-herald, who appears at first to be similar to the human being, except formed in gigantic stature. Yet, although he is so similar to human beings, his form is shadowy, as though he were a mere outline of the human being. He warns that without the appropriate seriousness, no one should seek entry into that which exists on the other side of the yawning abyss. We shall get to know this Guardian ever more and more in the following Lessons. The earnest Herald entreats us to be earnest.

And then, when we hear that voice and have understood it with appropriate seriousness, we should be aware of how, in abstractions, quietly, very softly, guidelines resound to us from across the threshold, which are meant to give us orientations from the spiritual realms. The threshold yawns before us and these quiet indications from the Guardian are meant to hold us back, lest we take a careless step. The voice of the Guardian resounds thus:

> From the expanses of space
> which in light acquires existence;
> from the pace of the course of time,
> which in creativity has its efficacy;
> from the depths of the heart's feeling,
> where, in the self, the world establishes its being -
>
> **There** is resounding in soul-language,
> **there** is glowing, from spirit-thoughts,
> from divine healing-forces in
> the Powers who form the world,
> creation's surging, efficacious Word -
> O, you human being, know yourself.

I will read it again:

> From the expanses of space
> which in light acquires existence;
> from the pace of the course of time,
> which in creativity has its efficacy;
> from the depths of the heart's feeling,
> where, in the self, the world establishes its being -
> **There** is resounding in soul-language,
> **there** is glowing, from spirit-thoughts,
> from divine healing-forces in
> the Powers who form the world,
> creation's surging, efficacious Word -
> O, you human being, know yourself.

With these words we can become clear how the secrets of existence must be fathomed from all that which exists and stirs in the depths of space and which from the depths of space manifests. How there must be fathomed a true knowledge, that which can manifest as a creative activity in the pace of the course of time. And how everything which manifests in the depths of the human heart as the world, has to be open to earnest seeking of the soul. For all of this is what can alone create the basis for that fathoming of one's own self which the student needs for enlightenment; for the fathoming of one's own self, wherein the cosmos however, has placed the entirety of its secrets. On the basis of this, human self-knowledge can be found from out of this Self; from this can be found all that which the human being needs in days of both health and illness, on his or her existential path between birth and death, and what a person will also have to use on that other existential path, the one between death and a new birth.

But all those who consider themselves members of this School should be clear, really clear, that everything that is not acquired in the mood and attitude {described above}, is not real knowledge, but only external, apparent knowledge. These people need to realize that what usually is regarded as knowledge, and taken up by people, before a person has acquired an awareness of the Guardian of the Threshold's admonitions regarding spiritual knowledge, is only apparent knowledge. But it need not remain only apparent knowledge. We do not regard this {earthly} knowledge with contempt. But we must be clear about this: that such knowledge then emerges from the stage of being only apparent knowledge, when it is transformed by all that which the human being can learn about the purification of his being, about the metamorphosis of his being, this is acquired by a person when he or she understands what the Spirit-herald is warning about at the yawning abyss of knowledge. This person needs to understand what this Spirit-herald, shining forth out of the darkness, is warning about, by calling out to human beings, on behalf of the finest spiritual inhabitants of the spiritual world.

Whoever does gain an awareness of the fact that between the sojourn in the fields of sense, wherein we must live between birth and death, and that which exists on spiritual realms, there is placed a yawning abyss, can achieve true, real knowledge. For only by means of this consciousness can the human being enter into true, real cognizing. Such a person doesn't have to become clairvoyant, although knowledge from the spiritual world is acquired by true clairvoyance. But he or she must acquire an awareness of what exists as a warning at the yawning abyss of the secrets of space, of the secrets of time; the secrets of the human heart itself. For whether we go out into the wide expanse of space, the abyss is there; or whether we journey forth into the cycles of time, the abyss is there; or whether we enter into the heart itself, the abyss is there. And these three abysses, they are not three abysses, they are a single abyss.

For if we go forth out into space so far that we come to where the expanses of space end, we find the spirit; if we go forth in the cycles of time to where they originate at the beginning of their cycles, if we go forth into the depths of the human heart, as deep as we can fathom ourselves: these three ways lead to only one goal, to one last end-point, not to three different places. They all lead to the same divine spiritual reality that wells forth from the primal fountain of the cosmos, which from the primal fountain of the cosmos fructifies and nourishes all being, and which also teaches human beings to discover the foundation of all existence; to recognize this.

In such earnest awareness we shall, in thought, place ourselves there, where the earnest Spirit-herald speaks, and we shall listen to what is understood as the particular conditions of our times, that is, as hindrances which we have to sweep away, in order to come to true spiritual cognizing. Hindrances to a spiritual cognizing, my dear friends, have existed in all times. In all times people had to overcome this and that, and put aside this and that, according to the warnings of the earnest Guardian at the threshold of the spiritual world. But there are obstacles peculiar to each age. What proceeds from human civilization is to a large extent not a help, but rather, a hindrance to us entering the spiritual world. And precisely from what emerges as the particular obstacles from each earthly civilization, and which are implanted in human nature by that very civilization, **this** is what the human being must put aside before he or she can cross the yawning abyss, which we have been referring to. Therefore let us now hear the earnest, watchful Herald of the gods, speak about this:

Yet, you must be aware of the abyss,
or else its beasts shall devour you,
as you hurry past me;
your earthly time has placed these in you
as the enemies of intuitive cognizing.

Behold the first beast, the crooked back,
bony is its head, of withered body;
its skin is entirely of dull blue;
your <u>fear</u> of spiritual creator-beingness
created this monster in your will;
only your courageous spiritual cognizing overcomes it.

Behold the second beast, it snarls
in a distorted countenance, it lies in its derision,
yellow with grey streaks is its body;
Your <u>hate</u> of the revelation of the spirit
created this weakling in the emotions;
the fire of your spiritual cognizing must overcome it.

Behold the third beast; with cleft snout,
glassy is its eye, languid is its posture;
its form appears to you as dirty red.
Your <u>doubt</u> in the power of spiritual light
created this spectre in your <u>thinking</u>;
it must yield to your creating of spiritual cognizing.

Only when the three are conquered by you
shall your soul grow wings
to carry you across the abyss,
which separates you from
the realms of spiritual cognizing
to which your heart
– seeking its well-being –
wishes to consecrate its yearnings.

I will read this again:

Yet, you must be aware of the abyss,
or else its beasts shall devour you,
as you hurry past me;
your earthly time has placed these in you
as the enemies of spiritual cognizing.

Behold the first beast, the crooked back,
bony is its head, of withered body;
its skin is entirely of dull blue;
your <u>fear</u> of spiritual creator-beingness
created this monster in your will;
only your courageous spiritul cognizing overcomes it.

27

Behold the second beast, it snarls
in a distorted countenance, it lies in its derision,
yellow with grey streaks is its body;
Your <u>hate</u> of the revelation of the spirit
created this weakling in the emotions;
the fire of your spiritual cognizing must overcome it.

Behold the third beast; with cleft beak,
glassy is its eye, languid is its posture;
its form appears to you as dirty red.
Your <u>doubt</u> in the power of spiritual light
created this spectre in your <u>thinking</u>;
it must yield to the calling forth of spiritual cognizing.

Only when the three are conquered by you
shall your soul grow wings
to carry you across the abyss,
which separates you from
the realms of spiritual cognizing
to which your heart
– seeking its well-being –
wishes to consecrate its yearnings.

These, my dear friends, are the three greatest enemies of spiritual cognizing for our times, for contemporary humanity. (*Regarding the First Beast*) The human being of today is afraid of the Spirit's creator-being-ness. Fear sits deep down in the soul. And he or she would like to deceive himself or herself that it is not there. One clothes the fear in all kinds of specious arguments, through which one tries to refute spiritual revelations. You will hear from this or that side, my dear friends, this or that argument against spiritual knowledge. It is sometimes clothed in clever, sometimes in sly, sometimes in foolish logical rules. But the logical rules are never the reason why spiritual knowledge is refuted. The truth is that it is the spirit of fear, existing deep into humanity's inner life, and working away, and which when it rises to the head, metamorphoses into logical reasons. It is **fear**!

But we must be really clear about this: it is not sufficient for us to say: I have no fear. Everyone can of course say that. We must first really comprehend the basis and the nature of this fear. We must tell ourselves that we were born and educated from within the present times, in which, from the Ahrimanic side, spirits of fear have been instilled, and that we are infected by these spirits. And by deceiving oneself that they are not there, doesn't mean that they really have gone. We must find the ways and the means – and this School will provide guidance for this – regarding these spirits which exist as monsters in our will, to have the cognitional courage with regard to them. For it is not what often leads people to cognitional awareness nowadays – or what they say provides them with cognitional awareness, but rather courage alone, the inner courage of soul which takes hold of the strength and the capacity to follow the path that leads to true, genuine, light-filled spiritual knowledge.

Regarding the Second Beast, which creeps into the human soul from the spirit of the times, to become an enemy of cognition: this beast lurks everywhere we go – it confronts the human being today in most of the literary works of our times, in most of the art galleries, in most sculpture and other artworks, and in music of all kinds. It guides its 'non-being' into the schools and in society; it is everywhere, in people's course of life. The second beast feels itself inwardly aroused to encourage mockery of spiritual knowledge, so that people do not have to acknowledge their fear of the spirit. This mockery is not always openly expressed, because people do not bring to consciousness what is within them. But I would say that only a thin wall, thin as a spider's web, separates the consciousness of the head, from what is in their hearts, wanting to ridicule true spiritual knowledge. And when the ridicule comes to light, this is when the more conscious, or less conscious, impertinence of modern man is able to suppress the fear. But basically, every person today is impelled to oppose the spirit's revelations, through remarkable forces in their inner nature. And this ridiculing, this mockery, manifests through the most extraordinary means.

Regarding the Third Beast: this is lazy, slack thinking. It is that comfortably convenient thinking which would like to make the entire world into a cinema; a cinema because one then does not have to think {one becomes a passive observer}, where all the images are reeled off before you, so that one's thinking {i.e., consciousness} only has to follow what is being reeled before your eyes. In this same way in fact, modern science would like to assess the external, physical world with this passive thinking[13].

The human being inwardly is wanting a comfortable life too much, to bring his or her consciousness (i.e., thinking) into a really active state. Today it is, with regard to consciousness, as if a person, if they want to pick up something from the floor, stands there with his hands in his pockets and thinks he can pick the thing up that way. But he cannot. And likewise, existence cannot be comprehended by thinking which has its hands in its pockets limply by the side. We must stir ourselves, must move our arms and hands if we want to grasp something from the floor, and we must activate our thinking if we want to comprehend the spirit.

The Guardian of the Threshold characterizes the first beast, which lurks as fear in your will, as a beast with a crooked back, with a countenance distorted into a skeletal appearance, and withered body. This beast, with a skin entirely of dull blue, is in actuality that which rises up from the abyss, placed alongside the Guardian of the Threshold, for modern humanity. And the Guardian of the Threshold makes it quite clear to the humanity of today: there it is, this beast in dull blue, with crooked back, and with a countenance distorted into a skeletal appearance. This beast is actually within you. It rises up there, from out of the yawning abyss which exists in front of the fields of higher cognizing; and it forms, as if in a kind of mirror, that which lurks in you yourself, as one of the enemies of higher cognizing; that particular enemy of cognition which lurks in your will.

And the second beast, which is connected to the enjoyment of mocking of the spiritual world, is characterized by the Guardian of the Threshold in a similar way. Alongside the other beast, it emerges, but in its posture it shows itself to be a weakling. Its posture is one of laziness, of slackness. But with its slack, lazy appearance, and grey-yellow body colour, it bares its teeth in a distorted countenance. And out of this baring of its teeth, which wants to laugh, but in laughing is lying, because the mockery in it is actually lying, it grins back at us, as the reflection of the beast that lives in our own feeling and, as the enemy of spiritual knowledge, hinders our search for higher cognizing.

And the third beast, which does not want to approach all that is in the physical world in spirit, the Guardian of the Threshold characterizes this as emerging from the abyss, with cleft beak, glassy eye and dull look, because its thinking does not want to be active; and with languid posture and dirty red form. Thus is this beast the lying Doubt which comes to expression through the cleft beak, which manifests, in the dirty red of its entire form, doubt in the power of spirit-light. This then, is the third of the enemies of cognition that lurks within us. They make us earthbound. {*See illustration 1 and 2 which depict these three beasts, from the Goetheanum red window.*}[14]

If with these beasts, we approach spiritual-knowing, ignoring the Guardian of the Threshold's warning: the yawning abyss is present there. One cannot place oneself over it if one is earthbound {*in the thinking*}, nor with fear nor mockery, nor with doubt. One can only cross it when: comprehending in thought, the **spiritual element** of being {*of reality*}, when one has experienced, in feeling, **the soul** of being {*of reality*}, when one strengthens for one's will, **the efficacy** {*the enlivening power*} of being {*of reality*}.

---

[13] Passive here does include the normal analytical assessment, in contrast to engaging with the sensory impressions in an active, strenuously intuitive way, which would eventually open up an holistic awareness capacity.

[14] The author's *The Meaning of the Goetheanum Glass Windows*, explores the meaning of these windows.

Then shall the intelligence, the soul element, and the enlivening power of being (*reality*) for our will, become wings which raise one above the weight of the earth. Then we can cross over the abyss.

Threefold are the stages of prejudice, which cast us into the abyss, if we do not acquire cognitional courage, cognitional fire and cognitional creativity. If, however, we do acquire cognitional courage in thinking. and want to activate this thinking; if we do not wish to approach the spirit in slovenly lassitude, but receive the spirit with inner fire of the heart, and when we have the courage to really comprehend the spirit actually as spirit, instead of letting it approach us as something material, in {*mental*} images, then shall the wings grow which will carry us over the abyss, where every human heart, which is honest with itself today, yearns to be.

That is what, my dear friends, this first introductory lesson wishes to bring before your souls, by means of which, and with which, this School for Spiritual Science begins. In conclusion, let us review once more the beginning, middle and ending of the experiences with the Guardian of the Threshold.

(The verses are repeated, and the Lesson ends with the following paragraph):

Concerning what is to be experienced in passing by the Guardian of the Threshold, what is necessary to experience in feeling, willing, thinking, in order to pass by the Guardian's light and to stride into the darkness from out of which that light shines in which we recognize the actual human Self - as to this, in the next lesson we shall hear more. In the next lesson, we shall hear of that which manifests out of the darkness, which shines out from the Spirit, illumining the darknesses.

German text of VERSE for Lesson 1   (part one)

Wo auf Erdengründen, Farb' an Farbe

Sich das Leben schaffend offenbart;

Wo aus Erdenstoffen, Form an Form,

Sich das Lebenslose ausgestaltet;

Wo erfühlende Wesen, willenskräftig,

Sich am eignen Dasein freudig wärmen;

Da betrittst du deines Eigenwesens

Tiefe, nachtbedeckte kalte Finsternis;

Du erfragest im Dunkel der Weiten

Nimmer, wer du bist und warst und werdest.

Für dein Eigensein finstert der Tag

Sich zur Seelennacht, zum Geistesdunkel;

Und du wendest seelensorgend dich

An das Licht, das aus Finsternissen kraftet.

Und aus Finsternissen hellet sich –

Dich im Ebenbilde offenbarend,

Doch zum Gleichnis auch dich bildend,

Ernstes Geisteswort im Weltenäther,

Deinem Herzen hörbar, kraftvoll wirkend –

VERSE for Lesson 1   (the deeper, initiatory level, part one)

Where in spirit-distant earthly places,

colour upon colour manifests,

calling forth existence;

Where, from earthly matter,

form upon form gives shape and texture

to the Inanimate;

Where resolutely, Beings with dim inner awareness,

through their own existence, happily warm themselves;

Where you, O human being, acquire for yourself

corporeal existence, from earth and air and light:

There you enter your own being's

Deep, cold darkness, enveloped in night;   1

You enquire never, in the dimness of space's wide

expanse,

Whom you are, and were, and shall become.

For your own being, day darkens

to soul-night, to spiritual dimness;

and, in anxiety of soul, you turn towards the light

which is empowered from out of the darknesses.   2

And for you out of darknesses there brightens –

yourself revealing in exact likeness,   3

yet forming you into an allegory also –   4

an earnest spiritual signifier, in the cosmic ether,   5

audible to your heart, powerfully efficacious:

German text of VERSE for Lesson 1, part two

Dir der Geistesbote, der allein

Dir den Weg erleuchten kann;

Vor ihm breiten sich die Sinnesfelder,

Hinter ihm, da gähnen Abgrundtiefen.

Und vor seinen finstern Geistesfeldern,

Dicht am gähnenden Abgrund des Seins,

Da ertönt sein urgewaltig Schöpferwort:

Sieh, ich bin der Erkenntnis einzig Tor !

Aus den Weiten des Raumeswesen,

Die im Lichte das Sein erleben,

Aus dem Schritte des Zeitenganges,

Der im Schaffen das Wirken findet,

Aus den Tiefen des Herzempfindens,

Wo im Selbst sich die Welt ergründet:

Da ertönet im Seelensprechen,

Da erleuchtet aus Geistgedanken

Das aus Göttlichen Heileskräften

In den Weltengestaltungsmächten

Wellend wirkende Daseinswort:

O, du Mensch, erkenne dich selbst.

VERSE for Lesson 1   (part two)

The Herald of the Spirit –

whom alone can illumine the path for you,

In front of him, spreads out the fields of the senses,

Behind him, there yawns the depths of the abyss.

And before his darkened fields of the spirit,

at the edge of the yawning abyss of being,

there resounds his most powerful Creator-Word –   6

*"**Behold, I am the only portal to spiritual cognizing** !"*   7,8

(The Guardian now speaks)

From the widths of space   9

which in light acquires existence;

from the pace of the course of time,

which in creativity has its efficacy;

from the depths of the heart's feeling,

where, in the self, the cosmos establishes its being –

<u>There</u> is resounding in soul-language,

<u>there </u>is glowing, from spirit-thoughts,

from divine healing-forces in

the Powers who form the world,

creation's surging, efficacious Word –

O, you human being, know your self.   10

Commentary and Notes for Verse One

1 "Deep, cold darkness enveloped in night": this spiritual darkness is the result of the sensory or earth-bound cognitive state of lines 1 & 2: the illusion of "colour upon colours calling forth existence" (that is, the physical world), and the illusory drive to be "happily warming oneself".

2 "the darknesses": this remarkable plural expression is referring to the several veils that encompass and darken consciousness: the mineral-material substance of our body and also the etheric and the astral energies, or substances, which, subject to both Luciferic Ahrimanic influences, cloud the awareness of incarnate people.

3 "exact likeness": in this phrase, the German word here for 'likeness' also has another meaning, namely 'a double'.

4 "Allegory": is the most accurate translation here, because the image is also an allegory, not a 'spirit-likeness' or 'ideal image', etc, for this has already been said. Although usually an allegory is a narrative, rather than a graphic image, 'allegory' here provides the correct meaning to this line, and is a specific usage found in 18th & 19th century German literature. The noun used here satisfies the specific grammatical circumstances to have the special meaning of, 'allegory'. An allegory is a literary device wherein you describe something, by using another, quite different, but very appropriate description, in words or in a complex graphic image, etc. So it is similar to a metaphor, but it is more substantial than that. Thus, the 'pearl of great price' is a metaphor for the Kingdom of the Heavens; whereas, the actual story of the Prodigal Son is an **allegory** presenting the journey of the soul from the lower state to seeking redemption. For the spectral image of our soul which the Guardian produces, to be called an 'allegory', implies that within this form, in the appearance of this being, is condensed a significant story – namely, the karma of the acolyte.

Also Plato's account of the soul as a charioteer whose carriage is drawn by a black and a white horse, is an allegory of the lower and higher souls. So, to the newly developing clairvoyance of the acolyte, the Guardian reveals his or her Double. And this figure is an exact likeness, but not as a photographically true reflection of our bodily appearance. It is an exact portrayal, in astral imagery, of the inner reality of the self, especially of the Luciferic and Ahrimanic traits; not of the physical face. In the ugly traits of the image there is also 'a story' (a detailed presentation) of the qualities of the Double.

5 "cosmic signifier": as we noted earlier, the usual translations have 'cosmic word', but such a choice carries the limiting nuance of audible speech.

A note about some key German terms
(There is also a glossary at the back of the book)

Welt: translated often as 'world'
This word is usually translated as the world, but this word can mean: the universe, Creation in general, or the planet Earth, or the environs in which a person lives (that part of the planet (actually, the hemisphere) which a person experiences and interacts with, in their daily life. Thus in the Soul Calendar, 'Welt' almost always means 'hemisphere'. There are four different meanings of this world, "Welt".
the earth: if only that part of the planet on which a person is living, i.e., the local environs around about us, is meant
the Earth: if our planet as a whole is meant
So, in a First Class verse, the word 'Earth' and the word 'earth' could both occur, each with their specific meaning.
the cosmos: this translation is used if the 'universe' is meant; that is, the Earth and the Moon's forces, as well as the planets and also possibly, the zodiac.
Creation: this translation means a slightly lesser view of the universe than 'cosmos', that is, the Earth and the Moon, (with perhaps the planetary spheres and the zodiac implied.)

Ich, and Selbst: translated as 'I' and 'self'
When the every-day, earthly ego is meant, these words are usually translated as 'I' or 'self'. When the higher, spiritual ego is meant, these are translated as higher I or Higher-self.

Geist: mind, spirit, intelligence, soul
As will be pointed out in the verses, this word does not always mean 'spirit'. So in the same verse, it could mean 'intelligence' and also, elsewhere in the verse, 'spirit'. For in the German world, the word 'Geist', meaning our intelligence, is understood (at least in anthroposophical literature), to derive from beyond the material world; thus either from the Soul-world or Devachan. The task of the translator is to discern whether it is being used to mean our intellect or a higher intelligence derived from beyond the material plane.

Spirit/soul
The word 'spirit' really means true, actual 'spirit' that is, the higher aspect of human nature (or of the cosmos) which derives from Devachan, not the astral realm. As such, this word is not the same as 'soul', which derives from the astral realm. Often in non-esoteric literature, these two meanings are not so clearly defined, but where the German word 'Geist' occurs in the 19 verses, I endeavour to reflect its actual meaning of 'Devachan'; however there are a few places in the Class Verses where it can refer to the common usage of 'intelligence'.

Commentary: VERSE for Lesson 1, part two,   (page one)

6 "Creator-word": the German could also possibly mean, 'creative-word'.

7 The term, 'portal' can be either door or gate or portal, these are the three meanings of the German word (Tor). If used for 'gate' it means normally a prosaic gate. But here the meaning is a larger opening in a barrier or wall, such as a grand temple door.

8 'spiritual cognizing' means 'spiritually discerning': usually translated as 'knowledge', which is grammatically correct. Now, the German word, 'Erkenntnis', in normal usage means either, cognition, knowledge, or discernment; however in philosophical or spiritual texts it has a specific meaning. Rudolf Steiner explains in detail that if used about higher truths, it means a higher knowing; a 'spiritual discernment' or intuitively perceiving. So it means, a definite spiritual cognizing, bordering on clairvoyance, a meaning found in the works of Goethe and Spinoza. Rudolf Steiner taught that to Spinoza, the human mind has a highest mode of discernment, or of knowing (Erkenntnis), which is in effect a 'spiritual discernment'. He defines Spinoza's use of this term as 'anschauende Wissen'; which translates as 'an intuitive knowledge'.
Goethe described this as "a cognizing which conveys to a person more than what sensory cognition discovers". So it means 'intuitive (clairvoyant) cognizing'. I have used 'spiritual discerning', or 'spiritual knowing' or 'spiritual cognition', depending on the context. One doesn't need to pass by the Guardian to gain 'knowledge', if knowledge means conceptual knowledge of spiritual realities, for these are accessible in books. But it is necessary to go pass the Guardian to gain one's own intuitive cognition of spiritual realities.

9 "the widths of Space": the phrase (in German, 'der Raumeswesen') means, "the beings of space". But to me, an error exists in the German; for it should read 'des Raumeswesen'; which means simply, 'space'. In 1924, Rudolf Steiner was unwell; some errors were made. He might correct these when giving that same Lesson on a later occasion; and there were also changes to the verses, which are improvements he decided to make. Also in his private notebooks, there are variations to the accepted official texts. With regard to "the expanses of space", only one letter needs to change, (der to des) for the singular, more consistent, impersonal, meaning of 'space', and not "the beings of space". Actually the expression "Raumeswesen" occurs only about ten times in all of his 4,200 lectures, and in these, the meaning is always 'space' not 'beings of space'. That the usual version is an error, and "the expanses of space" is meant, is also seen in the fact that this phrase in the verse, parallels the Prelude verse, which refers to the expanse of space, as well as to the flow of time; these are referred to as inanimate fundaments of our physical world. Crucially, in the Class lesson itself, Rudolf Steiner refers to 'der Raumeswesen' twice, without any mention of spirit beings; it is simply refers to inanimate space. So this phrase is really, the 'expanses of space' (inanimate space) not 'beings' of space. Furthermore, 'time' here is also presented as just an inanimate fundament of earthly life.

In Lesson 8 is an example of a similar error. In some official publications, the German has „Menschenwollen sich verwandeln" (that is, 'human will transforms'), which is the correct spelling of the verb (**verwandeln**). This is also in the English Class book, of 1994, and in various privately made versions. However, in the official German Class book, the actual spelling in the original Class transcripts is retained: **verwandlen.** But no such verb existed as of the 20th century; for it is a very old, rare version of *verwandeln* and came into existence in the 15th century, some two centuries later than the usual version (*verwandeln*), then it died out about 1844. It cannot be proven, but the version 'verwandlen', is almost certainly an error. Fortunately in this case, the two words mean the same thing, so the intended meaning of the verse is not affected. As we shall have to note later on, there are also errors in the spelling of the Greek name of the 'Mights'; these will be corrected in the relevant places.

Commentary: VERSE for Lesson 1, part two, (page two)

10 **"Know yourself"**: that is, intuitively cognize/discern your earthly self, including the Doubles; and yet it is also implied here, to intuitively come to experience your Self, (the higher, cosmic Self).

A note about the Double and the Guardian

Looking at these lines again,

> And out of the darknesses there brightens
> revealing yourself in exact likeness
> yet also forming you into an allegory –
> an earnest spiritual signifier in the cosmic ether,
> audible to your heart, powerfully efficacious.

It is important to note here that this verse is extremely condensed, creating an especial demand that it be focussed upon meditatively, for it implies both the Lesser Guardian and the Greater Guardian. There is firstly, through a psychic vision, a perceiving of an earnest spiritual signifier, namely, the Double. This is indicating accurately, but allegorically, one's hidden imperfections, perceptible to the Guardian. But gradually this astral form has brightened into visibility, or rather, one's astral body is now sufficiently purified to shed some light out into the immediate astral environment, so to speak.

So the Double is something which is both psychically seen, and inwardly felt. But this process is brought about by the Lesser Guardian. Our Double, and thus the intentions of the Lesser Guardian, is resounding in the ether. 'Spirit signifier' seems better here than 'spirit word' (which implies some form of speaking), because this manifesting to the meditant of the astral form of the Double, is a psychic vision, not so much a spiritual speaking (a transferring of thought-forms to the meditant).

But one can say **metaphorically** that this vision still does 'speak' to the meditant. Remember the term 'word' is just a surrogate for the subtle impact of the outer reality upon our consciousness. We are told that our inner sensing is detecting this form. So it is both a psychic (visual) experience and also is a subtle, soundless signifying of what all this means. But then in this part of the verse, it is indicated, without any break at all in the narrative, that the Guardian, called the Herald of the Spirit, is somewhere behind, and thus responsible for, the appearing of this Double.

> The Herald of the Spirit – whom alone
> can illumine the path for you.
> in front of him, spreads out the fields of the senses....
> ....there resounds his all-powerful Creator-maxim:
> 'Behold, I am the only portal to spiritual cognizing.'

So now, here, very subtly, the Greater Guardian, no longer the Lesser Guardian, has become the focus of the verse. And from now on in the Class Lessons, the verses will be concerned with the Greater Guardian.

Note:

The Greater Guardian is an Archangel, who places a veil over the spiritual realms, meaning Devachan, to give protection to human beings, as they may not consciously experience these divine realms until they have achieved a degree of spiritual development. This being exists at the upper level of the seventh astral plane, at border of Devachan.

The Lesser Guardian is a being who protects us from the Lower Self, the Double.

German text of VERSE for Lesson 1 (part three)

Doch du mußt den Abgrund achten,

Sonst verschlingen seine Tiere

Dich, wenn du an mich vorübereilt'st;

Sie hat deine Weltenzeit in dir

Als Erkenntnisfeinde hingestellt.

Schau das erste Tier, den Rücken krumm,

Knochenhaft das Haupt, von dürrem Leib,

Ganz von stumpfem Blau ist seine Haut;

Dein Furcht vor Geistes-Schöpfer-Sein

Schuf das Ungetüm in deinem Willen;

Dein Erkenntnismut nur überwindet es.

Schau das zweite Tier, es zeigt die Zähne

Im verzerrten Angesicht, es lügt im Spotten

Gelb mit grauem Einschlag ist sein Leib;

Dein Haß auf Geistes-Offenbarung

Schuf den Schwächling dir im Fühlen;

Dein Erkenntnisfeuer muß ihn zähmen.

Schau das dritte Tier, mit gespaltnem Maul,

Glasig ist sein Auge, schlaff die Haltung,

Schmutzigrot erscheint dir die Gestalt;

Dein Zweifel an Geistes-Licht-Gewalt

Schuf dir dies Gespenst in deinem Denken;

Dem Erkenntnisschaffen muß es weichen.

VERSE for Lesson 1   (part three)   (the Guardian speaks further:)

Yet, you must be aware of the abyss,

or else its beasts shall devour you,

as you hurry past me;

your earthly time has placed these in you

as the enemies of spiritual cognizing.

Behold the first beast, the crooked back,

bony is its head, of withered body;

entirely of dull blue its skin;

your **fear** of spiritual creator-beingness

created this monster in your will;

only your courageous spiritual cognizing overcomes it.

Behold the second beast, it snarls

in a distorted countenance, it lies in its derision,

yellow with grey streaks its body;

Your **hate** of the revelation of the spirit

created this weakling in the emotions;

the fire of your spiritual cognizing must subdue it.

Behold the third beast; with cleft snout,

glassy is its eye, languid its posture;

as dirty red its form appears to you.

Your **doubt** in the power of spiritual light

created this spectre in your thinking;

when spiritual cognizing is attained, it must yield.

German text of VERSE for Lesson 1 (part three, cont.)

Erst wenn die drei von dir besiegt

Werden Flügel deiner Seele wachsen,

Um den Abgrund zu übersetzen,

Der dich trennet vom Erkenntnisfelde,

Dem sich deine Herzenssehnsucht

Heilerstreben weihen möchte.

VERSE for Lesson 1 (part three, cont.)

Only when the three are conquered by you

shall your soul grow wings

to carry you across the abyss,

which separates you from

 the realms of spiritual cognizing

to which your heart's longing

 – seeking its well-being –

wishes to consecrate itself.

****

Commentary: VERSE for Lesson 1, part three

These three Beasts are actually depicted in the great Red Window of the Goetheanum, created years before the First Class was given. The magnificent window was probably first seen about 1918. A questioner asked Rudolf Steiner around 1920, some years before the First Class came into being, 'Whether they were in fact the shadow side of thinking, emotion and will'? His response was, "*Ensure that you make no abstract scheme of this, otherwise you block your access to these things. These creatures are realities, not abstract thoughts*". This reply affirms that the Red window depicts what is described here as the Three Beasts, in the First Class lesson (which was not yet given), but that one should not think abstractly about them, for they are allegorical depictions of real **entities**, not mere symbols. He obviously discerned that the questioner was caught up in this kind of theoretical thinking. (The conclusion that Rudolf Steiner denied that these Three Beasts are depicted in the Red window, in his answer, is incorrect.)

The fine poetic reflections upon these three Beasts by the pioneering anthroposophist, Wilhelm Rath, contains a number of inaccuracies. In particular he has incorrectly identified the central figure, the long bony form, as representing the negative emotions. But this figure actually depicts the evil shadow side of our **will**, not of our feelings. These windows contain initiatory secrets of the highest order, and disclose their secrets to esoteric consciousness as the self-initiation process develops for the acolyte. They are a very valuable adjunct to the discipline of undertaking the meditative exercises.[15]
See Illustrations 5 and 6 on pages 157,158.

1 The correct rendering here is "your earthly time", not your **cosmic** time. The meaning is that, as from mid-Lemurian times onwards, when humanity began to incarnate, and thereby ceased its existence in cosmic spirit realms, and descended into the material body, the Lower-self developed. The Double began to be accreted, or rather drawn into our soul, into our ether body and later, into the material substances of our physical body. And in particular, it is the inner soul nature of the current earthly time – from the middle of the 4th Post-Atlantean age, into the 5th Post-Atlantean epoch – which allows the 3 beasts to develop their influences within one's attitude to the spiritual. So this is an important correction to the common translation; you can read more about the cosmic Age when the Ahrimanic Double arose in my, *The Lost Zodiac of Rudolf Steiner*, this book also has illustrations designed by Rudolf Steiner depicting the lower elemental forces of the primordial Double.

---

[15] See this author's *The Meaning of the Goetheanum Windows*, for a clear explanation of the scenes carved into them. Illustration 6 shows the the three Beasts of the Red window; these have been especially coloured to show their link to the First Class.

German text of VERSE for Lesson 2

Des dritten Tieres glasig Auge,

Es ist das böse Gegenbild

Des Denkens, das in dir sich selbst

Verleugnet und den Tod sich wählet,

Absagend Geistgewalten, die es

Vor seinem Erden leben geistig

In Geistesfeldern lebend hielten.

Des zweiten Tieres Spottgesicht,

Es ist die böse Gegenkraft

Des Fühlens, das die eigne Seele

Aushöhlet und Lebensleerheit

In ihr erschafft statt Geistgehalt,

Der vor dem Erdensein erleuchtend

Aus Geistesonnenmacht ihr ward.

Des ersten Tieres Knochengeist,

Er ist die böse Schöpfermacht

Des Wollens, die den eignen Leib

Entfremdet deiner Seelenkraft

Und ihn den Gegenmächten weiht,

Die Weltensein dem Göttersein

In Zukunftzeiten rauben wollen.

VERSE for Lesson 2

The third Beast's glassy eye –   1

it is the evil counter-image

of thinking – a thinking which in you   2

denies itself and chooses death;

rejecting spirit-powers which spiritually

kept it alive in spiritual realms

before its earthly existence.

The second Beast's mocking countenance –

it is the evil counter force of the emotions,

which hollows out the soul, and in it

creates emptiness of life, instead of

spiritual content which once it had,

illuminating it before its earthly existence,

from might of the Spiritual-Sun.

The first Beast's skeletal psyche –   3

it is the evil creator-might of the will,   4

which alienates your own body

from your soul's forces, and dedicates it

to the opposing Powers, who intend

to rob world-being from the gods in future ages.   5

Commentary: VERSE for Lesson 2

1 **"glassy eye"**: in each of the three verses, the primary feature of the forms of the beast in question represents the beast itself, its quintessential qualities.

2: **"of the thinking – a thinking which"**: it is especially important to understand the subtle meaning of the verse here, and this is helped by repeating the word, 'thinking'. The common translations could be clearer here. This is because the subject of the verb "is" in the 2nd line, is the glassy eye. But the subject of the verb 'denies itself' in the 4th line is 'thinking', **not the glassy eye**. In other words, materialistic thinking denies its existence inside the consciousness of the human being (it does not deny the allegorical glassy eye). Like Ahriman himself, materialistic thinking tries to hide itself from the human being's awareness. The verse does not mean that the evil counterpart of thinking denies itself to itself, but it hides itself **from us**, from our earthly consciousness. It is the task of the meditant to awaken to the full reality of the subtle materialistic thinking or attitudes which incarnate people naturally tend towards.

3 The beast's **"skeletal psyche"**: other translations ('ghostly skeleton'/'bony ghost', etc) don't really convey the subtle esoteric meaning. The German term here, 'Knochengeist' means _something_ is bony or skeletal. But what is this _something_ ? The something here is called "Geist"; this word is often mistranslated in anthroposophical literature. This word has some six meanings to a German person; that of an astral entity or higher spiritual being is a much less common meaning in German literature. Its primary meaning is that of consciousness or mind, in the normal humanistic sense (except in texts where a spirit-entity is the subject).

   Though this is a text about spirit-beings, here this astral entity is not being referred to yet again as an astral entity, because that would be quite unnecessary. That has been made clear already. Rather the focus is the beast's chief characteristic – namely, that its inner-nature (or consciousness or mind-set) is 'bony'. You may prefer to use 'skeletal mind' or 'bony consciousness' or 'skeletal soul-nature'. The actual meaning of the phrase, a 'bony psyche' needs to be meditated upon; but in general terms, it refers to the intrinsic quality which hardened mineral matter has, to subdue one's spiritual holistic consciousness, and to invoke earth-bound volition.

4 **"evil creator-might"**: this phrase can also be rendered as 'evil creative-might'.

5 **"world-being"**: this unusual phrase as part of this line, means that malignant spirits seek to take part of Creation and make it in into an 'anti-cosmos'; using some of the etheric and astral and even Devachanic elements of our human nature. The corresponding presence of these in the spiritual counterpart of the solar system are what Ahriman and Lucifer seek to transform into a malignant reality. But if the line said simply 'world', this could mean only the Earth is meant; if it said 'cosmos', this would tend to ignore the Earth as part of what is meant. But 'world-being' allows the Earth, and its associated cosmic aspects to be included.

Further Thoughts about the Three Beasts

On the left is a clumsy, heavy bird. One gets the impression that this bird cannot fly; and its eyes are glassy and empty. This figure graphically presents the kind of thinking which is 'earthbound', that is, an attitude of mind which is not able to accept spiritual ideas. Such thinking rejects ideas about everything beyond the material world, especially spiritual realms and spirit beings. So this figure is depicting **doubt** in the existence of spiritual realities.

The entity on the right slightly resembles a human being; it has prominent teeth and dead, wiry bits of hair. It is about the lower un-spiritual, unclean desires and emotions. In particular, it depicts the soul-state in which **hate** of spirituality, and of spiritual realms, dominates. This kind of soul-state hates the existence of high morality, of purity, of a kind, selfless, warm-hearted way of feeling. For all of these imply the end of its self-centred life and indulgence in lowly pleasures. This state of soul makes people express their antipathy to spirituality in a veiled way. They become sarcastic about spirituality; they want to mock it. And where there is hate, there is usually fear; these two qualities are interlinked.

But when the emotions are so imprisoned in a lowly ego-centric state, the result is that the intellect becomes too predominant, so the emotions then shrivel up. This person can be very clever, but their emotional life eventually suffers under the influence of Ahrimanic thinking; this can lead to physical illnesses and mental health problems. The teeth are the most hardened part of the body, and therefore here they are huge; this presents artistically the emotional capacities being dulled and hardened through the self-centred, lowly desires and feelings. Likewise the deadened hair represents an unwise, un-spiritual consciousness, illustrating anthroposophical understanding that our hair is the result of spiritual energy streams condensing into matter; if the hair becomes so hardened and deadened, then one's consciousness has likewise become deadened.[16]

Finally, in the middle of the three, is the largest and most powerful of the negative soul qualities: evil or anti-social **Will**. In this negative force, there is **fear** of the good, of the spiritual, and thus a rejection of social conscience, a lack of interest in the needs of other people. The form of the third beast is a masterly artistic portrayal (or metaphor), of the anti-social will. We see a hardened being – it is quite bonelike – with almost no limbs; except that it has four small legs. They remind us not of a human being, but of animals, so this is then 'the Beast' in the human being; a human being who has potent fear of the spiritual, of the Divine. For our will is operative in us through our limbs; here the limbs are tiny, and very significantly, the upper limbs, that is, our arms and hands, are absent here.

Although this entity is not a person, it does represent a negative human reality; so we can say that it is making a powerful statement about the hidden, shadow-side of the human being, of the will: a hidden, unethical will, in effect, not true will at all; it has no organs to manifest our normal, decent will. It is an artistic meditation on 'anti-will', or the non-existence of that good will which is at the core of every decent human being. We need to note too that where there is fear of something, there is often hatred of it as well.

Also, we have another limb or organ for our will – the jaw and mouth, through which we speak. This power to speak, to create language as a vessel for our thoughts, is in many ways the highest expression of human consciousness or will. This beast has no mouth; it is unable to speak. It has no part of the divine Logos, who spoke Creation into being, and whose influence is subtly active, deep in the human being, as the core of our spirit.

---

[16] GA 117, lects. 22nd Nov. & 7th Dec. 1909.

Note: Structure of the VERSE for Lesson 3

In commenting on Lesson 3, Rudolf Steiner emphasized that each of the three verses has a specific metre or underlying structure of stressed and unstressed syllables. A 'stressed' syllable is also referred to as 'long'; the 'unstressed' syllable is referred to as 'short'.

Rudolf Steiner's German verses have a very clear metrical structure, but it is difficult to achieve this in translation, without choosing English words that are either awkward, or which don't convey the specific nuances of meaning of the German equivalent. My translation attempts to provide this metrical quality, but included also is my other translation which is clearer in meaning, but which lacks the important underlying rhythm.

For the verse about **thinking,** the appropriate metre is the 'trochee', or trochaic metre: it is long, short / long, short, thus creating a falling effect: ‾ ~ ‾ ~ ‾ ~ ‾ ~

For the verse about **emotions,** the appropriate metre is the 'iambus', or iambic metre: it is short, long / short, long, thus creating a rising effect: ~ ‾ ~ ‾ ~ ‾ ~ ‾

For the verse about the **will,** the appropriate metre is a 'spondee', or spondaic metre: the syllables here are all equally stressed — — — —

Note:
This verse is presented in two versions. Firstly, a metrical version; that is, the rhythmical structure of the lines corresponds to the metrical form which Rudolf Steiner stipulates it should have. But in his various commentaries on this verse (there were three occasions when this happened), he gave different interpretations to one line in particular.

So the verses for Lesson Three are given again (after the German original) in a form which does not maintain this metrical form, but adds two extra lines to include the additional meanings, and also attempts to more clearly convey the nuances of the German words.

German text of the VERSE for Lesson 3

Sieh in dir Gedankenweben:

Weltenschein erlebest du,

Selbstheitsein verbirgt sich dir;

Tauche unter in den Schein:

Ätherwesen weht in dir;

Selbstheitsein, es soll verehren

Deines Geistes Führerwesen.

Vernimm in dir Gefühle-Strömen,

Es mengen Schein und Sein sich dir,

Die Selbstheit neigt dem Scheine sich;

So tauche unter in scheinendes Sein:

Und Welten-Seelenkräfte sind in dir;

Die Selbstheit, sie soll bedenken

Der eignen Seele Lebensmächte.

Laß walten in dir den Willens-Stoß:

Der steigt aus allem Scheineswesen

Mit Eigensein erschaffen auf;

Ihm wende zu all dein Leben:

Der ist erfüllt von Welten-Geistesmacht;

Dein Eigensein, es soll begreifen

Weltschöpfermacht im Geistes-Ich.

VERSE for Lesson 3

‒ ~ ‒ ~ ‒ ~ ‒ ~

See in you the weaving thoughts:

cosmic semblance now you undergo*   (*= experience)

selfhood-being hides from you;

in the semblance submerge yourself:

ether-being is stirring in you;

selfhood-being shall revere

your own mind's guiding Beings.

~ ‒ ~ ‒ ~ ‒ ~ ‒

Perceive in you the streams of feelings:

the semblance and being is mixed in you,

the selfhood tends towards the semblance;

So submerge in seeming being;

and cosmic powers of the soul are in you;

the selfhood – it should ponder well

the soul's own powers of life.

‒ ‒ ‒ ‒ ‒ ‒ ‒ ‒

Let reign in you the thrust of will;

it arises from all semblance

with its own being's creative might.

Turn towards this all your life;

filled it is with cosmic spirit-might;

your own being – it should take hold of

Cosmos-Creator power in the spiritual I .

VERSE for Lesson 3 (non-metrical version)

See in you thoughts forming, interweaving;	1
you are experiencing world-illusion,	1b
selfhood-being is hidden from you;	2
immerse yourself in the semblance:	
the ether is flowing actively within you;	3
selfhood-being, it should revere –	
the divine Beings guiding your intelligence	4
the ether-body's guidance of your intelligence	5
the guiding actions of your Guardian Angel	5b
Perceive streams of feelings in yourself:	6
semblance and real being is blended in you,	
Selfhood tends towards the semblance;	
So immerse yourself in seeming being;	6b
and cosmic soul-forces are in you;	7
Selfhood – it should reflect on	
it own soul's powers of life.	8
Let prevail in you the thrust of the will;	
which arises, creative, with its own being	
from out of all semblance.	
Turn towards this all your life;	9
it is filled with cosmic spirit-might;	
your own selfhood – it should take hold of	
Cosmos-Creator power in the spiritual I .	

Commentary: VERSE for Lesson 3

These Notes refer to the wording of the non-metrical version. Its meaning is clearer, but it lacks the correct rhythms, which both support and convey the meaning, on the feeling level. Note that in my version, this Verse has two extra lines, because Rudolf Steiner gave three meanings to one line (see #4).

Core lesson: start to realize, to experience, that behind the normal personality's thinking, feeling and will, there lies veiled, much deeper, more spiritual manifestations of these.

1 thoughts "interweaving, forming": this seems more accurate than simply 'weaving'. The verb used here by Rudolf Steiner (weben) is very often used by him, and although one of its meanings is 'to weave', there a second meaning to this verb: 'producing', 'bringing-forth', 'tracing out', etc. So the meaning here is 'inter-weaving', in the more substantial sense of free-flowing, ongoing producing of thought-forms.

Regarding the metrical version: "...**now you undergo**" (*experience) – the correct verb here is 'to experience', as in the non-metrical version, but this verb cannot fit in the metrical structure of the line.

1b "world-illusion": the term "Welt" (world) can mean our planet Earth, or the cosmos, or the general environment around about us; this third meaning is meant here. The world we encounter around us, and analyse in our thinking, is being referred to as an illusory thing, for this early verse is about normal, earthly, non-initiatory consciousness, which is illusory in comparison with initiatory consciousness. This is defined as 'Maya' in Oriental terminology.

2 'selfhood-being is hidden': it is literally, 'selfhood-*being*' or 'selfhood *existence*', but this additional word (being) is primarily needed for the metre.

3 "the ether is flowing actively within you": here the meaning is that **the etheric is actively moving** as a result of us using our thinking; especially our higher thinking processes. The German literally here has 'ether being-ness', which means in effect 'etheric substantiality'. But the additional German word for being-ness (Wesen) is added in order to give the right metre. So one could say here, 'Ether energies are moving in you'. They need not be thought of as gently wafting; that is a possibility, but is not necessarily the case.

4, 5, 5b "the guiding Beings of your intelligence"
   "the ether-body's guidance of your intelligence"
   "the guiding actions of your Guardian Angel"
Usually this line is translated as **"your spirit's guiding Beings"**, and as a line having only one meaning; but Rudolf Steiner gave it three meanings.

But firstly, we note that the word "Geist" occurs here in German, which is referring to our mind or intelligence, because this portion of the verse is about one's thoughts. The German word (Geist) can mean either 'mind' or 'spirit'. Secondly, we note that a word in this verse, (Führerwesen) grammatically can be either singular or plural, and in fact this was used in both a singular and a plural way by Rudolf Steiner.

* **"the guiding Beings of your intelligence"**: in Lesson 3 (29. Feb. 1924), he referred to it as plural, and as referring to a number of spiritual beings, identified as the hierarchical beings, who guide the advancing meditant into cosmic awareness. The implication here is that these spiritual beings are assisting the meditant to enter into a kind of thinking which is tending towards 'Psychic-Image consciousness' (traditionally called "Imagination"). That is, a consciousness experienced when the mind or intelligence can perceive thought-forms present in the ethers.

Commentary: VERSE for Lesson 3   (cont)

* **"the ether-body's guidance of your intelligence"**
But in a Recapitulatory Lesson (Prague, 5. April 1924) Rudolf Steiner explained it as being singular, and as referring to the meditant's consciousness, when functioning beyond the earthly rational thinking, in the ether-body; thus into 'holistic' or Psychic-Image consciousness. This is similar to the above, but with the major difference in Rudolf Steiner's words that, as a singular word it means,

> . . the physical body only gives us that which is dead semblance; whereas the etheric body is where we first have a thinking (i.e., a consciousness) which rises above the semblance (i.e., above logical, rational earthly thinking)"...whoever properly feels how earthly thinking is only the corpse of {their} pre-conception spirit-soul nature, such a person gradually feels themselves to be **primarily an etheric being**....such a person is aware that they must be able to **revere this etheric-beingness**.

* **"the guiding actions of your Guardian Angel"**
Also, in a Recapitulatory Lesson Three, given on 11th Sept. 1924, Rudolf Steiner identified this phrase as meaning one's Guiding Angel, "...then we come to revere at least that Guiding Being who guides us from life to life."   (p.51, German edition of 1977)

6 "Perceive streams of feelings": in effect, "discern the presence of streams of feeling", but note that the verb here has also the nuance of an inner hearing of these energies.

6b "seeming being": this is simply another way of saying 'semblance'. or illusion or Maya.

7 "cosmic soul forces": that is soul-forces from the cosmos; in particular, from the planets.

8 "Powers of life": here the term, 'life' means the primary feelings that are our emotions, and which can manifest with great intensity; these are the astral influences from the planets.

9 "Turn to this all your life": that is, throughout all of your life, turn to this. This phrase in the German is ambiguous, and grammatically can also mean; 'devote (or apply) all of your life('s energies) to *this*; i.e., to the will, in its best nature. However, the verse means that the meditant should allow the best will-forces to prevail in herself or himself. So the meditant is urged to let the real will, not the illusory will, (thus not illusory ambitions), prevail in their life. It is not a matter of devoting one's life to the better will, but rather that one's will **is *now to be visualized as*** this better, higher will: this process gradually assist one's will to becomes the higher will. Then one's life naturally embodies the higher will.

German text of the VERSE for Lesson 4

(Der Hüter spricht)

Fühle wie die Erdentiefen

Ihre Kräfte deinem Wesen

In die Leibesglieder drängen.

Du verlierest dich in ihnen,

Wenn du deinen Willen machtlos

Ihrem Streben anvertrauest;

Sie verfinstern dir das Ich.

Fühle wie aus Weltenweiten

Göttermächte ihre Geisteshelle

Dir ins Seelenwesen leuchten lassen.

Finde dich in ihnen liebend,

Und sie schaffend weisheitwebend

Dich als Selbst in ihren Kreisen

Stark zum gutes Geistesschaffen.

Fühle wie in Himmelshöhen

Selbstsein selbstlos leben kann,

Wenn es geisterfüllt Gedankenmächten

In dem Höhenstreben folgen will

Und in Tapferkeit was Wort vernimmt,

Das von oben gnadevoll ertönet

In des Menschen wahre Wesenheit.

VERSE for Lesson 4

(The Guardian speaks)

Feel how the depths of the Earth
push their forces into your being –
in the body's limbs.
You lose yourself in them
if powerlessly you entrust
your will to their endeavours:
for you, they darken your I . 1

Feel how, for you, from cosmic expanses 2
divine Powers let shine into the soul
their spiritual radiance.
Find yourself in these as loving,
that they, bringing forth wisdom, create
you as a Self in their spheres,
strong for good spiritual creating.

Feel how in heavenly heights
self-being can exist selflessly, 3
when, spiritually-filled, it wills 4
to follow Powers of Thought
into the striving up to the heights,
and in courage discerns the Word
which, full of Grace, resounds from above 5
in the human being's true nature.

Commentary: VERSE for Lesson 4

Core lesson: continuing on from Lesson 3, the meditant is urged to strive to perceive the cosmic spiritual reality behind the threefold soul.

The verses from this lesson form a meditation on our own inner 'cosmic-cross' which underlies many of the lessons. That is, the relationship we have to spiritual forces which are efficacious from below, (the interior of the Earth), from the horizontal plane (the planetary spheres) and from above (the zodiac).

1 **"depths of the Earth"**: this verse points one's attention to the earth-bound desires and interests which are strengthened from Ahrimanic energies in the caverns and subterranean depths of the Earth's interior. Forces surging up from below, the lower part of the cosmic-cross, exert their efficacy on the will. The more intensely they influence the earth-ego, the less of the radiant, higher ego is present.

2 **"from cosmic expanses"**: in a Recapitulatory Lesson, Rudolf Steiner told his audience that the Guardian here is directing our attention to forces which surge and hover, coming in from the four directions of the compass. So this middle verse is about the influences of the planetary spheres; the horizontal bar of the cosmic cross. The feeling capacity, broadly defined, is the area of their influence. (Whereas the third verse focuses on the upper part of the world cross; that is, the energies radiating down from the zodiac.)

3 **"self-being"**: (in normal English it should be 'selfhood'). The German here is literally 'self-being'; the purpose of this unusual expression is to contrast a state of having selfhood, the state of a more separate, earthly 'self-being-ness', with the selfless-ness of the higher ego.

4: **"spiritually-filled, it wills**...": this phrase can also mean, "when it wills to follow spiritually-filled thought-Powers..."

5: **"Grace"**: this term refers to the free deeds of love by Christ, and usually it is used by Rudolf Steiner to indicate how Christ's deeds enable the development of the Life-Spirit. But here it refers to a more general outcome of the Salvation deeds of Christ, namely that the old, higher consciousness which Lucifer removed and brought us into an Ahrimanic mind-set, can be re-developed, although in a new way.

We human beings can begin to spiritualize ourselves, and this starts with the striving for intuitive or holistic thinking, of becoming attuned to those cosmic thought-forms which underlie the shape and characteristics of all things in the physical world. Thus the verses of this lesson point the way to becoming released from the empty, matter-bound state of mind which the Prelude Verse has highlighted as modern humanity's special problem.

German text of the VERSE for Lesson 5

Es kämpft das Licht mit finstren Mächten

in jenem Reiche, wo dein Denken

In Geistesdasein dringen möchte.

Du findest, lichtwärts strebend,

Dein Selbst von Geiste dir genommen;

Du kannst, wenn Finstres dich verlockt,

Im Stoff das Selbst verlieren.

Es kämpft das Warme mit dem Kalten

In jenem Reiche wo dein Fühlen

Im Geistesweben leben möchte.

Du findest, Wärme liebend,

Dein Selbst in Geisteslust verwehend;

Du kannst, wenn Kälte dich verhärtet,

Im Leid das Selbst verstäuben.

Es kämpft das Leben mit dem Tode

In jenem Reiche, wo dein Wollen

Im Geistesschaffen walten möchte.

Du findest, Leben fassend,

Dein Selbst im Lebensmacht verschwinden;

Du kannst, wenn Todesmacht dich bändigt,

Im Nichts das Selbst verkrampfen.

VERSE for Lesson 5

The light battles with dark powers
in that realm, where your thinking seeks
to penetrate into spiritual existence.
You find, striving towards the light,   1
your self taken from you by the spirit;   1b
You can, if darkness tempts you,   2
loose the self in matter.

The Warm battles with the Cold   3
in that realm, where your feeling seeks
to exist in the spirit-interweaving.
You find, loving the warmth,   4
Your self drifting away in spirit-pleasure;
you can, if coldness hardens you,   5
disintegrate the self in pain.

Life battles with death   6
in that realm, where your will seeks
to be active in spiritual creativity.
You find, taking hold of life,   7
your self in spirit-might disappearing;   8
You can, if death's might subdues you,
cramp the self into nothing.   9

Commentary: VERSE for Lesson 5

Core Lesson: All three verses in this lesson are concerned with the dynamic that can still be experienced by the meditant when crossing the threshold; namely the inherent tendency to be attracted to either a Luciferic or an Ahrimanic way of functioning. It is about how these two Powers fight for the soul in regard to: Light & Darkness in thinking, Warm & Cold in feelings, and Earth-divorced will & Earth-bound will in regard to our volition.

1 "striving towards the light": it is vital to realize that here the meaning is about an influence upon the soul, drawing it towards Luciferic powers, not to Christ-associated light-power. In his commentary Rudolf Steiner refers to these Powers as trying to imbue the soul with many spiritual capacities, but without the human being itself making any effort towards a higher spiritual chasteness, to inwardly qualify for these. These Luciferic spirits, we are told in the Lesson, dwell in the Earth's atmosphere; this will be in the Light-ether layer, some 50-85 kms above the ground. (See my *Rudolf Steiner Handbook* for the structure of the Earth's atmosphere, spiritually viewed).

1b "self": the normal earthly self is meant in all of this verse, not the higher 'Self'.

2 "if darkness tempts you": here the meaning is, one is drawn towards a subtly ahrimanic way of thinking, not an obviously ugly darkness. Ahriman can tempt a developing spiritual seeker to take up a sinister interest in gaining personal power over others. (Both points 1 and 2 are elucidated in the Mystery Plays.)

3 "the warm": the verse says here not, 'the warmth', but 'the warm'.

4 "loving the warmth": again in a Luciferic sense.

5 "if coldness hardens you": again, in a subtle Ahrimanic sense, wherein the feeling-life is too self-centred, and a cold, enhanced intellectuality develops. Rudolf Steiner refers to the ahrimanic beings who cause this, as having "an immensely high intellectuality".

6 "Life battles with death": this verse is the most difficult of the three, and only a brief explanation of it is given in Rudolf Steiner's elucidation – deliberately, as it concerns the mysteries of the will, which are especially veiled. But from his brief comments in Lesson Five, and in a Recapitulatory Lesson, it becomes clear that here the focus is on two sets of beings, just as in the above verses. The word 'life' refers to Luciferic powers who would absorb us into their own egoistic intentions; they seek to "carry out their will in the cosmos, from **within our will**".[17] And 'death' refers to meaningless, materialistic activity.

7 "taking hold of life": this phrase (in German '...Leben fassend') is correctly translated in this way. But since human beings would not usually dissolve away into a Luciferic state if they 'take hold of life", the word 'life' has to be understood in a very different way. From Rudolf Steiner's commentary, it is clear that the meaning of 'life' here is not the wholesome normal sense. The single word 'life', which is without any other qualifying words, is used because it is serving as a pointer to various spiritual dynamics. One of these dynamics involves the influence and aims of Luciferic beings, whom Rudolf Steiner called 'powers of life' in the Lesson. So this phrase has a very specific meaning: that the meditant is being tempted by Luciferic urges to get away from normal earthly life. So the soul is "taking hold of" this temptation. As we noted above, it is the endeavour of such

---

[17] Page 75, German text, Vol. 3, 1977, Recapitulatory Lessons.

Commentary: VERSE for Lesson 5 (cont)

beings to take over our will, and merge us into their glowing, sparkling, self-absorbed indulgent goals.[18] Another reason for the use of the word 'life' is that this also points our attention to 'esoteric chemistry' remarks in the commentary from Rudolf Steiner when he gave Lesson Five. He spoke about the role of oxygen and nitrogen, as carriers of astral influences from Luciferic and Ahrimanic beings.

8 "**spirit-might**": some translations have here "powers of life" or "life-might". It is clear that this phrase does refer to the Luciferic beings, called simply 'life' in line 1 and line 4 of this section of the verse (see note 6). Also in the Recapitulatory lesson, Rudolf Steiner uses this phrase "powers of life" when referring to this line in his commentary, but despite speaking this, he retains 'spirit-might' in the verse. So, 'powers of life' is not correct to the actual text of the verse, but it is correct to the meaning of this line.

9 "**cramp the self into nothing**": the commentary in Lesson Five refers to this line saying, "The person then wants to unfold their deeds in 'death', that is, wants to undertake actions in 'death', {*meaning*} in nothing-ness." That is, to be active during life in pointless, materialistic activity. So, just as in the lines above, "life" means the Luciferic spirits, so here, "death" is not meant in the usual sense, but rather it points to Ahrimanic spirit beings, referred to by Rudolf Steiner as "powers of death". He reports in a Recapitulatory Lesson, that these beings endeavour "to weave our Will, for eternity, into forms made of matter".

Illustration 7 on page 159 is a pastel drawing by Rudolf Steiner which may be helpful here.

---

[18] There is also possibly a suggestion here, because the German phrase is so condensed, that 'life' i.e., Luciferic influences, are seizing the human being; then a reversed meaning - "life taking hold" - might possibly be implied. Also the phrase "**loving the warmth**" might be suggesting that the 'warmth' i.e., the Luciferic beings in the warmth forces, are reaching out, in a false 'loving' way to the human soul.

German text of VERSE for Lesson 6, part A

Du steigst ins Erden-Wesenhafte

Mit deines Willens Kraftentfaltung;

Betritt als Denker du das Erdensein,

Es wird Gedankenmacht dir dich

Als deine eigene Tierheit zeigen;

Die Furcht vor deinem Selbst

Muß dir in Seelen-Mut sich wandeln.

Du lebest mit den Wasserwesen

Nur durch das Fühlens Traumesweben;

Durchdring erwachend Wassersein,

Es wird die Seele sich in dir

Als dumpfes Pflanzendasein geben;

Und Lahmheit deines Selbst

Muß dich zum Wachen führen.

Du sinnest in dem Lüftewehen

Nur im Gedächtnis-Bilderformen;

Ergreife wollend Lüftewesen,

Es wird die eigene Seele dich

Als kalterstarrter Stein bedrohn;

Doch deiner Selbstheit Kälte-tod

Er muß dem Geistesfeuer weichen.

Verse for Lesson 6, part A

You descend into earthliness   1
with the unfolding of your will's power;
if as thinker you enter the realm of the earth –
power of thought shall show your self to you
as your own animality;
Fear of your own self must for you
transform into soul courage.

You live with watery nature   2
only through feeling's dreaminess;   3
awakened, penetrate watery being –   4
The soul shall show itself in you
as dull plant-existence;
and lameness of your self
must lead you to awakening.

You cogitate in the moving breezes   5
only in memory's imagery-forms;   6
with active will, grasp airy being –   7
Your own soul shall threaten you
as cold ossified stone;
Yet your selfhood's coldness-death
must yield to the fire of the spirit.

COMMENTARY: VERSE for Lesson 6, part A

Core Message: Lesson Six is about the subtle effect upon our consciousness of the elemental energies which underlie the realms of nature, especially in terms of subtle underlying Luciferic influences. Part Two of the lesson goes into this theme in more detail.

Note 1: This verse introduces the theme of an interweaving of our Will forces with those of our Thinking - this theme is more directly worked with in the verses for Lessons 7 and 8. In the first section, the 'animality' refers to the lower qualities in the human will, which is **something perceived by our thinking**, but which **is present in the will**. So, this section refers to the first Beast; we noted earlier, that this Beast has an animal quality, indicated by its four small legs. The last section is about the lower qualities in the human thinking which is something **perceived, indirectly by our will**, through its effect on us, when we attempt to 'live into' our **earthly thinking capacity** (which is sustained by the air element).

Note 2: each of these three verses is about the acolyte becoming more perceptive, and thus more able to discern, in a somewhat clairvoyant state, how they were unaware of the state of their inner life, especially with regard to the normal, unspiritual, influences operative in their etheric body. So here the acolyte is urged to discern this by being more alert to these influences. So, **"if as thinker you.."** means, as Rudolf Steiner explains in his commentary, if you assess your inner nature, especially your will-forces, *in a more alert way*, you shall see the Ahrimanic thinking tendency. And, if you also penetrate the water-ether or undines influences with a more alert, somewhat clairvoyant cognizing, then you will become aware of how dulled and dreamy or vegetative, those influences are. (It is not that you make the dulled slumbering condition awake, only then to find out that your soul is dulled down.) Thirdly, if you more clairvoyantly, or sensitively, assess your cogitating (thinking) process, you will discover how inwardly dead (or mineral-like) is the logical, intellectual activity.

1 **"You descend into earthliness with the unfolding of your will's power..."**
The usual translation, "Thou stridest into earthliness with thy Will's unfolding force" can give the wrong impression. For, when the person in Devachan, long after their past life has ended, seeks to be again an earthly human, the will is then unfolding, or making effective, its capacity to achieve just this aim. But this aim to become again an incarnate person comes about as a specific urge arises in the human being in Devachan: an urge which could be expressed as, 'I want to be a true human being again' – this is described by Rudolf Steiner in lectures on existence after death. So the will, in this phase, is inherently impelling oneself into earthly matter. Note the significance of this urge. It indicates that an inner alienation from the sublime Devachanic realms has arisen. This tells us that the capacity to retain consciousness of Devachan in the person is fading out, bringing perception of earth-bound interests, and the implication here is that our willing and our thinking are interlinked. So here, the influence of gnomes is being subtly referred to, and we need to note that gnomes can be subject to the influence of Ahriman.

So, it is not the case that the person descends and, as part of the process, their will obliges by getting suitably energized. Rather, the descent into matter is now the core intention of, and derives from, the soul's will; which means that all souls – apart from the few initiates who no longer seek immersion in the material plane – have an un-spiritual aspect to their will forces, which eventually impels them down to the Earth. By 'unspiritual' I mean, that from a very lofty perspective, Devachan should be, but is not generally felt to be, a suitable permanent home. It won't be until high initiation is achieved. This theme is related to a Gospel incident, the Transfiguration

COMMENTARY: VERSE for Lesson 6, part A (cont.)

scene, wherein St. Peter suggests to Christ that 'tabernacles' should be constructed; this means he is feeling the impetus to achieve the ability to dwell in Devachan. (Luke 9: 28-36) It is of course entirely right to want to reincarnate, if one is seeking to learn the lessons of earthly life, in order to develop one's spiritual potential. In the middle verse, the Double in the emotional energies is the focus. A more subtle awareness of one's feeling-life now brings perception of the lack of active commitment in the desires for the spiritualization process.

2 "**with watery nature**": this phrase is literally, 'with the being-ness of water', and here, as is made clearer in the next Lesson, the undines are involved.

3 "**feeling's dreaminess**": this phrase is literally 'feeling's producing/bringing-forth (or possibly, weaving) of dreams'.

4 "**penetrate watery being**": The meaning here is the acolyte should consciously assess, i.e., inwardly experience, the water-ether's condition (hence the undines), its influence in oneself; this will bring awareness of the tendency towards a dulled, unawakened state of all that is existing in the semi-conscious yearnings and general feelings. This is done as one awakens to the need to be awakened; It doesn't mean to 'send awakening through one's water-ether state' to then have the soul as a result, emerge, in a dulled condition.

5 "**You cogitate in the moving breezes**": the German verb 'sinnest' is not, "you sense in the moving air". The verb (sinnen) in more literary German, means to cogitate, not to sense something. And this is the meaning intended here, as Rudolf Steiner makes clear, "*the 'sinnen', an activity wherein we have predominantly to do with the memory-images...wherein one thought after the other occurs....in response to external actions...*" (First Class Vol 1. p.155, German edition) These are the mental images through which we process or assess our sense-impressions. So it also does not mean to 'dream' in the air-forces.

The meaning then is that in everyday life, our thinking-life functions simply as a processing of mental images, and in so doing uses the light-ether within the air element, (the air is permeated by light). This earthly type of thinking is all very rigid and non-intuitive; if one were to be immersed in this, it would have a hardening effect. This verse is also subtly referring to the influence of the air sprites or sylphs.

6 "**memory's imagery-forms**": if this is translated simply as 'memory's images', the German is not accurately expressed. Certainly our memory consists of images, but the German adds the word for 'forms' because then we are reminded that earthly thoughts in fact involve astral or etheric thought-forms. That is, the images in our awareness when are thinking, are not simply images which exist abstractly nowhere; on the contrary, they are realities. They exist as real, actual forms in our astral body and then in our etheric body. In Lesson 19 this idea of actual thought-forms as realities is referred to again, forming a central point in that Lesson.

7 "**with active will, grasp airy being**": as we noted earlier this is about our will indirectly perceiving the nature of our earth-bound thinking. This is confirmed by a First Class notebook entry of Rudolf Steiner's: "One can represent {to oneself this process as} the mineral element, being taken hold of by the Will".
{In his own words "*Man kann: Mineralisches als vom Willen ergriffen vorstellen*"}.

German Text of VERSE for Lesson 6, part B

Du hältst von Lichtes-Scheines-Macht

Gedanken nur im Innern fest;

Wenn Lichtesschein in dir sich selber denkt,

So wird unwahres Geisteswesen

In dir als Selbstheitwahn erstehn;

Besinnung auf die Erdennöte

Wird dich im Menschensein erhalten.

Du hältst vom Weltgestalten

Gefühle nur im Innern fest;

Wenn Weltenform in dir sich selber fühlt,

So wird ohnmächtig Geist-Erleben

In dir das Selbstheitsein ersticken;

Doch Liebe zu den Erdenwerten

Wird dir die Menschenseele retten.

Du hältst vom Weltenleben

Das Wollen nur im Innern fest;

Wenn Weltenleben dich voll erfaßt,

So wird vernichtend Geistes-Lust

In dir das Selbst-Erleben töten;

Doch Erdenwollen geist-ergeben,

Es läßt den Gott im Menschen walten.

VERSE for Lesson 6, part B

Of light's radiant power, you retain

Within you only thoughts;

If light's radiance itself **thinks** in you,   1

then false spirit-beingness arises   1b

as selfhood delusion in you;

Contemplating the Earth's afflictions   2

shall maintain you in human existence.

Of the 'world-forming', you retain   3

Within you only feelings;   4

If world-form itself **feels** in you,   5

then disempowered spirit experience

suffocates selfhood-being in you;

Yet love for the inherent merits of the Earth   6

will save for you the human soul.

Of the world's life, you retain   7

Within only the will;   8

if the 'world's life' fully **grasps** you,   9

then annihilating astral-pleasure   10

kills the experience of self in you;

yet earthly will, yielding to spirit,   11

allows the god in the human being   12

to actively exist.

COMMENTARY: VERSE for Lesson 6, part B

Core Lesson: Part Two concerns the subtle effect on our consciousness of elemental energies which permeate the ether layers in the Earth's upper atmosphere, especially Luciferic influences. See page 73 for the choice of 'world' instead of the usual translation, 'cosmic', in this verse.

(Point 1 refers to a major problem in the usual translations.)

1 "if light's radiance itself were to think in you"
The German here is ambiguous, and all other translations have opted for this possibility: **"if light's radiance were to *think itself* in you"**. In terms of grammar, this interpretation is based on a normal way of reading the word order of the sentence. But this results in a sentence which is much less meaningful, in fact almost meaningless; and which contradicts what Rudolf Steiner teaches in this Lesson, whereas my translation agrees with the commentary of Rudolf Steiner (see below). Quite often Rudolf Steiner uses an unusual word order, to emphasize his meaning; and he has done this here.

We note here that we can always say that something, 'stretches itself' or 'removes itself' or 'stops itself', etc; but to say that a radiant light can 'think itself' is confusing; it has no meaning. (There is only one similar strange phrase later on, in Lesson Seven: "you can will the intelligence", and this would be fully without any meaning, if Rudolf Steiner had not explained what is meant, which is very subtle indeed.) But here, his own brief comments in the Lesson show that my translation conveys his meaning.

Firstly, in his commentary, Rudolf Steiner teaches us that, in normal thinking, (which is really just mental pictures or representations), "*...the light is thinking in us. The light is what is thinking in us. When the light penetrates into us, it thinks in us.*"
He then proceeds to state, "*But in earthly life this light which {itself} thinks in us, is only semblance.*" (Here he is using the same phrase as is used in the verse, yet this is translated inconsistently, in the usual versions as, "which thinks itself in us".)

Secondly, Rudolf Steiner then teaches that as a meditant arises into an etheric-astral consciousness, such a person must develop a conscious, higher (holistic) 'thinking', that is, so-called 'Imagination' (or Psychic-Image consciousness). If they don't, then the astral light, which underlies normal illusory mental pictures, can unfold a Luciferic influence in the person.

He cautions in this Lesson that this **radiant astral (or 'spirit') substratum itself**, which 'carries' the thought that we experience, and which normally is the active force behind people's every-day thinking, **must not itself** exert any such influence in meditation. It is important that the Luciferic beings especially, are not 'thinking' in the meditant; rather the meditant herself or himself must only be experiencing higher, spiritual thinking.
That is why this line in the verse should read, as given above,
  "*If light's radiance itself **thinks** in you*"
and not the meaningless version,
  "If light's radiance thinks itself, in you".

My conclusion here is confirmed by the situation that Rudolf Steiner states this same thought in the Lesson three times, as we noted above. He is teaching in his commentary that if the light (the elemental energies in it) were itself to do the thinking in a meditant, then Luciferic beings, via Luciferic sylphs in the ethers, would manifest in the soul. The radiance of the light itself must not think in our soul; that is, whatever kind of consciousness exists in the various etheric-astral beings who are inherent in this realm, and from whom the light acquires its radiance, this must not manifest in our soul.

An example of Rudolf Steiner using an unusual word-order occurs in Lesson Nine, "*O human being....experience ...how for you, in existence, water-beings are shapers.*" Here the emphasis is on the powerful significance of water-sprites on we human beings **whilst we are in earthly existence**.

COMMENTARY: VERSE for Lesson 6, part B (cont)

1b "false astral-beingness": the German text literally is, 'untrue spirit' (or 'untrue astral being'). Again the word "Geist" is used, and again the meaning here is an astrality, rather than actual Spiritual (Devachanic) realities. So I have placed here 'astral' beingness, not 'spirit'-beingness, and also, in lines further down, "astral"-experience and "astral" pleasure; this is because these verses are referring to astral entities and their possible states of consciousness, so not Devachanic, divine states of being. Hence these verses don't refer to "spirit-beingness, etc". The translation, "untruthful' being" is less useful; for here a false or non-authentic astrality, derived from Luciferic influences, is meant.

2 "Earth's afflictions": people who are aware of the suffering of others, and seek to understand from empathy the cause of suffering, can protect themselves from Lucifer's appeal to selfish egotism.

3 "world forming": this means the influence present everywhere in the world from the tone-ether or water-ether, which gives characteristic forms to living things. Rudolf Steiner refers to the plant-world when he mentions this theme in the Lesson; hence he is also referring to the activity of the water-sprites or undines. This ether is what gives form, through presence of moisture, or lack of moisture, to objects; and this process in us and in nature is connected to Moon forces. But he emphasizes above all, the need to prevent Luciferic beings from having an influence in our meditating.

4 "retain within only feelings": the implication of this line is that the capacity of human beings to experience emotions, feelings and yearnings, is connected to the influence of the undines in the water-ether. But the inherent emotional astrality suffusing the water-ether is not part of our human astrality; we have our own. We can note here how our own feelings are expressed in our face by the changing of its form or shape; a process which is made possible by the fluid element of our body.

5 "world-form itself feels in you": and not as is usually said, "*world-form were to feel itself in you*". Just as with note 1 -"*If light's radiance itself **thinks** in you*", so too, here the meaning is that, energies from Luciferic elementals, are not to be exerting an influence in our consciousness. Rudolf Steiner on this point made a brief, definite statement, that we are not to "***carry along in us only feelings, which only the undefined (indefinite) 'world form' possesses***". The phrase "undefined world-form" may also refer to the masses of undines, who are described by Rudolf Steiner as 'cloud-like' and always metamorphosing; these are associated with the water-ether, and with plant-life. In a lecture of 3rd Nov. 1923, he told his audience how, as people leave their bodies in sleep, they pass through "*a 'sea of astrality' which is formed by the evolving, changing fluidic world of the undines, metamorphosing in all sorts of ways*". It is this background, and also Luciferic feelings, which the meditant is to rise above. The astrality pervading undines is a background element in humanity's feelings; this should not predominate in the soul. But especially Luciferic influences should not influence the meditating human being.

The water-ether provides the substratum of all the forms that objects take, in the physical world. The influence of the Luciferic undines active in this ether must not permeate and become our inner life, for this would suffocate the healthy earth-ego sense. This is a similar statement to the one above, but this refers to the feelings, rather than the thinking process. In earlier, times when people were not so deeply enmeshed in the body, this interplay of elemental energies or beings with human beings was perceived, to some extent. A startling reference to this capacity of the undines to influence our emotions is found from the 17th century, in official Swedish chronicles; "Many death certificates were issued during the seventeenth century, in which the cause of death of men was listed as "{sexual}involvement with a Skogsnurfva' {an undine}."[19] The word 'involvement' here means intense yearnings, caused by psychic visions of these beings, by Scandinavians who had 'second sight'. Although Rudolf Steiner's pastel drawing of the elementals is faded, one or two of the undines are depicted as attractive, alluring feminine forms.

6 "**inherent merits**": the translation, 'values' of the Earth is also accurate **if** this means in your mind the same as, 'inherent merits' of the Earth. But the translation, 'destinies' or 'mission' of the Earth are jumping ahead, beyond the German word (Erdenwerten), to what are further implications.

7 "**world's life**": this is a brief way of saying the aspect of the world which manifests as life, life permeated by Will, an intention pulsing through creation; an intention to actively be, to do something. The life of all living beings derives from the life-ether, in which the gnomes are active.

8 "**the will**": the first of these verses refers to our thinking, which is carried by the radiant ether-astral energies, the second to our feelings or emotions, this third section refers to the will. The term 'life' refers to life-ether, and the role of the gnomes in this ether, as they condense physical substances, in response to the Ideas of the cosmos, of gods. It is from the denser aspect of our body, especially the skeletal structure which lies at the core of our limbs, that we can manifest our own human will. The physical mineral world is an expression of the Will of divine beings.

9 "**world's life**": this is a very abbreviated way of saying the matter-forming (or "earthiness") power of gnomes, using the life-ether; these beings can be closely allied to Ahrimanic activity. The intentions resonating in the life-ether and carried out by gnomes, is not meant to swamp our will; it should not grasp or seize us.

10 "**annihilating spirit-pleasure**": if the impulse driving the beings responsible for condensing and sustaining physical creation, from out of the life-ether becomes our will – and the implication here is of somewhat Ahrimanically influenced beings – then their pleasure in fashioning physical-mineral objects, exerting an influence in our astral nature would destroy our sense of self.

11 "**earthly will, yielding to spirit**": here we see that the "spirit-pleasure" is an ahrimanic drive. If we let our life's priorities (i.e., our will) be oriented to the spirit, then this Ahrimanic influence is kept away.

12 "**god to actively exist**": the usual translations have 'hold sway' or 'rule', or 'prevail'; and this could in theory apply here. But the verb here (walten) also means 'to be active', or

---

[19] Nancy Arrowsmith, *A Field Guide to the Little People,* London: Pan, 1977, p. 98.

COMMENTARY: VERSE for Lesson 6, part B   (cont)

'to be'. The meaning is probably more that of 'being actively present' rather than an absolutely prevailing or ruling; can an acolyte in the early stages be described as having a divine volition always prevailing? A rare instance here of Rudolf Steiner using the word 'God', is preceded by his words, "*so that the Gods can actively exert their influence in us*" (15th Sept. '24), thereby merging the two ideas of 'God' and 'gods'.

This line is about the hierarchies as such, active in our will. That Rudolf Steiner also uses the word 'God', is due to fact that our will, in its unfallen, highest mode (as Spirit-human or Atman) does have a higher, more divine origin than our feelings or logical thinking capacity. In fact, the will derives from the Being who is often (but not always) meant by the word, 'God': the highest of the Thrones. From this sublime and mighty Being, in the old Saturn Aeon, the germinal human will and our Atma were rayed forth, together with a rudimentary form of the physical body.

Cosmic or earthly ?
The usual translations have 'cosmic-forming' and 'cosmic life', whereas I have 'world-life' and 'world-forming'. In his Lesson, Rudolf Steiner made a simple diagram showing 7 layers:

world-life	(He is referring to the Earth's Life-ether layer)
world-forming	(He is referring to the Earth's Water-ether or Chemical-ether layer)
light	(The Light-ether layer is indicated)
warmth	(The Warmth-ether layer is indicated)
air	
water	
earth	

He referred to these layers as 'world' layers, as they are part of the Earth's structure. That is, our planet's upper atmosphere is enveloped in four layers of ethers. So here the word 'world' means our planet, not the cosmos.

But in the Lesson he briefly referred to 'cosmic elements' within the 'world-life' and 'world-forming' layers. He then identified these elements as Luciferic spirits; such beings are not offspring of our planet, so they can be called 'cosmic'. Therefore any layer affecting us is an ether-layer of our world (our planet), but one from which Luciferic spirits (from the cosmos) can be influencing us.
My *Rudolf Steiner Handbook* has a diagram which identifies the actual height and location of these layers, created from an analysis of upper atmosphere scientific research, and from another, more detailed diagram from Rudolf Steiner.

O, schau die Drei,
Sie sind die Eins –
Wenn Du die Menschenprägung
Im Erdendasein trägst.

Erlebe des Kopfes Weltgestalt

Empfinde des Herzens Weltenschlag

Erdenke der Glieder Weltenkraft

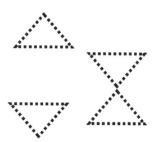

Sie sind die Drei,
Die Drei, die als das Eins
Im Erdendasein leben.

Des Kopfes Geist –
Du kannst ihn wollen;
Und Wollen wird dir
Der Sinne vielgestaltig Himmelsweben:
    Du webest in der Weisheit.

Des Herzens Seele,
Du kannst sie fühlen;
Und Fühlen wird dir
Des Denkens keimerweckend Weltenleben;
    Du lebest in dem Scheine.

Der Glieder Kraft,
Du kannst die denken,
Und Denken wird dir
Des Wollens zielerfassend Menschenstreben;
    Du strebest in der Tugend.

Tritt ein – das Tor ist geöffnet,
Du wirst ein wahrer Mensch sein.

VERSE for Lesson 7

Oh, behold the Three,
they are the One –
when you carry the human-form's imprint   1
into earthly existence.

Experience the head's cosmic form   2

Feel the heart's cosmic pulse

Think-out the limbs' cosmic power   3

They are the Three,
the Three, which in earthly existence
live as the One.

The head's intelligence –   4
you can *will* this;   5
and for you,
the polymorphous world of the senses –   6
wrought by the heavens –   6b
becomes **Will**:   7
your cognizing is imbued with wisdom.   7b

The heart's soul   8
you can *feel* it;   9
and for you, the seed-bud awakening cosmic life
of the heart's deeper awareness –   10
of thinking's willing, willing's thinking, imbued with feeling – 11
becomes **feeling**:   12, 12b
you are living in the radiant glory.   13

The limbs' power,
you can *think* it,   14
and for you willing's
purposeful human striving
becomes a higher **thinking**:   15
you are striving in virtue.   16

Enter – the door is opened,
you shall become a true human being.

COMMENTARY: VERSE for Lesson 7

Note 1: the verses in this lesson become clearer in Lesson 8; these two Lessons form a unity. Note 2: The usual translations of the verse for this Lesson are especially incorrect; this has meant that major changes have been needed for my translation.

1 "Human form's imprint": The German phrase is alludes to human form as if it were an imprint put upon the soul; created in the way that warm wax receives the design of a seal.

2 "...cosmic form": i.e., the head's oval shape derives from the oval-shaped cosmos.

3 "Think-out": that is, think about, really graphically think of, the presence of the cosmic energies in the will. There is an allusion here to the substrata of the earth below and how from this, spiritual energies stream out into one's limbs. This meaning is not specified here, but it forms an essential basis for the extended meaning, given in lesson 8.

4 "The head's intelligence": here most translations have "...*the head's spirit*" but this does not convey the meaning of the German. It is not the head's 'spirit' as such which is meant, because the German phrase refers to the faculty of conceiving ideas (concepts), and forming mental images. We know this because Rudolf Steiner himself defined what this phrase is about: "***the Head's 'Geist" – that is, its thinking***". (Recapit. Lesson 15th Sept. 1924, p.130, German edition). The commentary from Rudolf Steiner makes clear, our thinking is tied to what our twelve senses, our sensory capacities, reveal to us. This verse is offering us a way to realize the cosmic counterpart to our intellectual capacity or thinking ability.

The meaning here is not that willing becomes a thinking tied to the senses, but the opposite, our thinking activity becomes experienced as having an interface with will, with Divine will. The sense-world is a predominant focus of our thinking, but in meditation our higher, more intuitive cognizing reveals that behind this multi-formed, complex sense-world lies the will of its Creators. The normal activity of our thoughts is the evaluating of mental images, which themselves are derived from sense-perception. But when meditatively cognized, such thinking is a process which has a Will-element underlying it; it derives from the cosmos.

5 "you can *will* this": note that this is not a grammatical statement; so its meaning has to be inwardly grasped. It is suggesting that through a higher consciousness state, you can view or experience thinking as if it were closely associated with Will. See the commentary to Lesson 8 for more about this.

6 "polymorphous world of the senses" (i.e., multi-formed): this refers to the diverse forms of the sensory world. In his commentary, Rudolf Steiner told his audience (German edition of 1977, page 182), that the verse is about the sensory worlds: that is, the many diverse sensory experiences which our senses communicate to us.

6b "wrought by the heavens": that is, the sensory reality is wrought by, or brought about by, divine beings in the heavenly realms. The verse is indicating that the sense-world, with its many forms which we perceive, is the outcome of activity undertaken in the spiritual worlds, but manifesting in the sensory world. From Rudolf Steiner's general lectures, we can view these as deriving from the cosmos, and hence the zodiac, (and we can correlate this to our twelve-fold senses). The official version, "thousandfold heavenly weaving of the senses", fails to convey the intended meaning.

7 "becomes will": this refers to becoming aware of the intentions or cosmic-will behind the sensory inflow which the head, (our logical thoughts), constantly analyse; this is elaborated in lesson 8. These sensory realities become revealed as an expression of cosmic Will.

COMMENTARY: VERSE for Lesson 7 (cont)

7b "your cognizing is imbued with wisdom": an idiomatic German expression is used here which translates into English literally as, "You are weaving in wisdom". At times Rudolf Steiner did use 'weben' in this way – referring to a gentle, eurythmy-like movement. But this expression is also a German idiom, when the other meanings of the verb 'weben' are meant, other than 'to weave'. These meanings include, 'to bring forth', 'to be astir', 'to be very alive', 'to be in motion'. To use here the translation, "You are weaving in wisdom" is not so helpful, because here the implication is of a much more dynamic process occurring in the meditant's consciousness, **raising it up to a higher level**. The message is that the meditant has begun to cognize beyond earthly perception, into the etheric-astral realms. So cognizing is now very alive, wisdom-imbued, and hence is bringing forth to consciousness, awareness of spiritual realities, at least to some extent. My translation attempts to convey this meaning. If you achieve perception of the "Imaginative" cosmic intelligence behind Creation through your efforts, you perceive that this thinking has a Will quality permeating it. Then you are cognizing, and immersed in, the wisdom which, from the Gods, permeates Creation.

8 "The heart's soul": this term means the heart's deeper awareness, or the consciousness underlying our feeling-life, the core of the astral body. It is important to recall that this is described by Rudolf Steiner as deriving from the planetary spheres.

9 "you can feel it": that is, in a meditative state, you can attain to an enhanced feeling or perceiving of the quality of your core astrality ('the heart's feelings'), and then you discover it has a connection with planetary astrality.

10 & 11 Here we encounter a major difference in my translation: an additional line is inserted; this is because, in a Recapitulatory Lesson, Rudolf Steiner gave a second meaning to this line. We will now consider point 10, and then in point 11, the second meaning revealed by Rudolf Steiner.

10 "of the heart's deeper awareness": and not 'of the heart's thinking". Here as with the verse above this, the meaning is the opposite of what the usual translations can suggest. We are told that something becomes 'feeling' for the meditant: what is this? It is two things, but we shall leave aside for the moment the second aspect, and explore the verse from the commentary given in Lesson Seven. From that Lesson it is clear that this 'something' is what this verse starts with: the core of the verse, the 'heart's soul'. This obviously means the deeper qualities in the heart, that is, in our feeling-life. And here we encounter the difficulty that Rudolf Steiner does use the word 'thinking' for any consciousness state, whether the intuitive thinking or psychic-imaginative visions or higher clairvoyance. So the word 'thinking' which occurs in the usual translations, can be misleading here.
What is meant is not 'thinking' in the normal use of this word, but the deeper awareness, the more spiritually sensitive, spiritually-aware feelings that we can have as the spiritual-soul develops; in other words, the higher consciousness (or 'clairvoyant') awareness that our heart can experience. But in this middle verse, there can not be any swapping over, as happens with thinking into will, or will into thinking, in the first and the third verse. Instead, 'feeling' becomes more deeply 'feeling'.
Now that we have identified this 'something', we need to note that it is described as having a cosmic life in it, which is "seed-bud awakening". In other words, our deeper feelings or emotional capacities are linked to cosmic influences (the planets), and their influence in us can awaken the germinal seed-bud potential for a deeper, more meaningful life. It was in his remarks about this, that Rudolf Steiner refers to the 'Music of the Spheres' as resonating in our heart, but on a deeper, less conscious level. We noted also there are two 'somethings' which become 'feeling'– that is, which become discovered, as the deeper awareness, deeper consciousness of the heart, of the astral body; this second aspect is explored in note 11.

COMMENTARY: VERSE for Lesson 7 (cont)

11 "**of thinking's willing, willing's thinking, imbued with feeling**": this second 'something' is identified by Rudolf Steiner in a Recapitulatory Lesson to be both "thinking and willing". It is essential to realize that the word 'thinking' is now being used in the normal way here. He explains that the meditant, as clairvoyance develops, begins to perceive that this deeper astral consciousness in the core of the astral body, does ray out into our thinking and willing, (Prague 17th September, 1924 p.130). Rudolf Steiner then stated that this same line should actually (also) read as:
"***Thinking's willing, willing's thinking, becomes for you feeling: seed-bud awakening cosmic life***". His words in this commentary are brief, almost aphoristic, so one has to contemplate what they are really signifying. It appears that he means that the deeper aspect of our thinking, namely a will-force, and the deeper aspect of our willing, namely a cosmic thinking, are derived from the core of our astral body, (regarded here as our feeling-life), meaning here the deeper awareness capacity of the heart, the astral body.
We remind ourselves now, that on the first time that he gave Lesson Seven, this line was defined as, "***The heart's deeper awareness ('soul') becomes feeling: seed-bud awakening, cosmic life***"; so this second commentary implies that an additional line is needed in the verse to include this second meaning – this is given in my translation.

12 "**becomes feeling**": the cosmic quality in our deeper heart-consciousness, from the planetary spheres, is what the meditant with some developing clairvoyance, now experiences in their feeling-life.

12b "**becomes feeling**": and secondly, the feeling-life now becomes perceived as raying into the thinking and will.

13 "**radiant glory**": the exceptionally radiant nature of the cosmic intelligence living within the core astral consciousness, is experienced *as something divine which manifests itself*, not as a religiously emotive experience. Rudolf Steiner in his Gospel commentaries points out that "glory" has a more substantial and definite meaning than is usually understood, namely, that of a divine reality becoming manifested.

14 "**you can *think* it**": note that this is not a grammatical statement; so its meaning has to be inwardly grasped. It is suggesting that through a higher consciousness state, you can view or experience the will forces in the limbs, as a form of cosmic intelligence or cosmic 'thinking'.

15 "**becomes a higher thinking**": this is literally in the German, "becomes thinking", but this refers to the wisdom and cosmic thoughts behind the volition, and not to our usual logical, brain-bound thinking. This theme is further elaborated in lesson 8.

16 "**virtue**": the meditant becomes aware of the higher spiritual forces, cosmic 'thinking' or wisdom, active within our volition. This achievement then leads to an alignment of one's will to the higher will prevailing in spiritual worlds.

German text of VERSE for Lesson 8

Sieh hinter des Denkens Sinneslicht,

Wie in der finstren Geisteszelle

Wollen sich hebt aus Leibestiefen;

Lasse fließen durch deiner Seele Stärke

Totes Denken in das Weltennichts;

Und das Wollen, es erstehet

Als Weltgedankenschaffen.

Sieh in des Fühlens Seelenweben,　　　　　　　(Seelenwehen)

Wie in dem Träumedämmern

Leben aus Weltenfernen strömt;

Laß in Schlaf durch die Herzensruhe

Menschenfühlen still verwehen;

Und das Weltenleben geistert

Als Menschenwesensmacht.

Sieh über des Wollens Leibeswirken,

Wie in schlafende Wirkensfelder

Denken sich senkt aus Haupteskräften;

Laß durch die Seelenschau zu Licht

Menschenwollen sich verwandeln;

Und das Denken, es erscheinet

Als Willenszauberwesen.

VERSE for Lesson 8

See behind thinking's sensory light –

how in the darkened cells of spiritual intelligence   1

willing is rising out of the body's depths: 2

let, through your soul's strength,

dead thinking flow into cosmic nothingness,

and the will – it comes into being as

creation and herald of cosmic thoughts.   3

See in the feelings' meandering of soul –   4

how, in the dimness of dreams,

life is streaming in from cosmic distances:

let human feeling,

through the heart's tranquillity,

gently drift into sleep,

then cosmic life is astir spiritually

as the human being's inherent nature.

See above the will's activity in the body –   5

how, from the head's forces, thinking descends   6

into slumbering fields of activity.   7

Let, through the soul's perceiving,

human willing transform into light,

then thinking – it appears as

the magical capacity of the will.   8

COMMENTARY: VERSE for Lesson 8

Core lesson: this is a continuation of Lesson 7.

1 "darkened cells of spiritual intelligence": the usual version, "spirit-cells", is not helpful. The German text is a poetic phrase, which points to the spiritually aware intelligence or consciousness, which has to use the brain as its vessel. This consciousness does not exist as 'cells', but since the brain is constructed of many cells, all of which are meant to respond to thoughts arising in our soul, our spiritual consciousness (or thinking) is here described in a similar way. The verse is about how spiritual human forces (present, but hidden, in our will) exist behind our logical thinking when we are corporeal, incarnate people.

2 "willing is rising...": here we can begin to make more meaningful the phrase in Lesson 7 : one is "to *will* the thinking". Now we note that the "will", which is connected to thinking, actually refers to three things. One of these is the cosmic will-energy behind the interplay of the sensory process, and another is the will or intentionality that is always subtly present in acts of mental-imaging or conceptualizing. Then thirdly, after these realizations, we become aware that this meditative process leads on to awareness of the existence of a higher, not a brain-bound, 'thinking' i.e., to Psychic-Image consciousness (Imagination) as mediator of the wisdom existing as astral thought-forms in the astral plane. And this wisdom is experienced as both a will energy, as well as an insightfulness.

3 "creation and herald of cosmic thoughts": this line in the verse directs the meditant towards two interwoven dynamics active between the cosmos, and our consciousness, as perceived by Psychic-Image consciousness (or Imagination). However, Rudolf Steiner's commentary has only brief, suggestive comments, because his intention with this verse is that the meditant gradually acquires some grasp of this complex dynamic, or insights which come beyond logical thinking.

Meditation on this line leads to an awareness that, as abstract, dead thoughts are cast away, and higher perceiving is attained (Psychic-Image consciousness), the will becomes an active part of our cognizing; one result is that the meditant becomes aware intuitively of 'cosmic thoughts', which means the wisdom of the gods. So, as this happens, the will is not actually **creating** such 'cosmic thoughts' but bringing them to our awareness. The German text indicates this. For the verb used here, 'schaffen', which usually means 'to create', is used here in the same way as it is in Lesson One, where it is not referring to a 'creating'; but to a 'calling forth' or 'conjuring up' of something: hence, this meaning is '*calling forth* cosmic thoughts to our perception'. For, as this mysterious, intuitive force of the will is accessed in meditation, then this active power within the will makes possible the perception of cosmic thoughts. Our will is then a herald, to our consciousness, of cosmic wisdom.

But, as Rudolf Steiner's own commentary in the Lesson teaches, our will itself is the result of the creative power of the cosmic thoughts of the gods: hence, 'cosmic thoughts creation' is also a meaning of this line. Because, our will is the result of creative activity of spiritual activity of the gods, when they were forming the Ideas from which Creation arises.

4 "feelings' meandering of soul": the German text, 'weben', is usually translated as 'soul-weaving', but the verb also means to 'bring forth/produce/trace-out'. But, significantly, in his Lessons, Rudolf Steiner also used, as an alternative word, 'wehen', instead of 'weben'. This word means to be wafting/blowing/moving, in the manner of the wind; thus, apart from a 'weaving', (really, a 'bringing forth') there is also the nuance of feelings and moods arising as part of a meandering, changeable inner landscape; and so I have used the the phrase 'meandering of soul'.

COMMENTARY: VERSE for Lesson 8   (cont.)

5 "above the will's activity in the body": one's view is not directed to the limbs and their energized state, but to the head, to thinking. This is similar to the theme of verse One, wherein, when thinking is the focus, the view is directed not just to the head, but to the overall body (in which the will is present). Then one detects the presence of a spiritual energy, invoked by empowered, insightful thinking i.e., spiritually oriented conceptualizing, which has a radiance about it, and which descends from the head area, and permeates the will.

6 "thinking descends": this phrase refers not to the descent of logical concepts, but to spiritual energies which are related to the will, and which are present in our intelligence, in the forming of, or receiving of thoughts, especially spiritual holistic insights.

7 "slumbering fields of activity": the phrase refers to the various activities driven by our will – in a deeper, fuller sense of that word – within the body; activities, or more accurately, actions which are efficacious, but which are mainly subconscious; hence referred to as 'slumbering'. Much of the will, its influences in us, is beyond our conscious awareness, and therefore, relative to our thinking, is 'asleep' or slumbering. Only the initiated person can integrate these deep-seated, veiled, activities into her or his ego-consciousness.

8 "magical nature of the will": the capacity of the will is described as 'magical', referring to its natural ability to manifest in lightning-fast activity, and to tirelessly sustain the processes essential to our existence. This may involve decision-making in critical circumstances where action is needed without being delayed or clouded by intellectual or emotional factors; the will is also the mysterious force which drives the extraordinarily complex metabolic processes that underlie our digestion and our immune system.

German text of VERSE for Lesson 9

O Mensch, ertaste in deines Leibes ganzem Sein
Wie Erdenkräfte dir im Dasein Stütze sind.

O Mensch erlebe in deines Tastens ganzem Kreis,
Wie Wasserwesen dir im Dasein Bildner sind.

LEBEN

O Mensch, erfühle in deines Lebens ganzem Weben,
Wie Luftgewalten dir im Dasein Pfleger sind.

O Mensch, erdenke in deines Fühlens ganzem Strömen,
Wie Feuermächte dir im Dasein Helfer sind.

O Mensch, erschaue dich in der Elemente Reich !

LIEBE O Mensch, so lasse walten in deiner Seele Tiefen
Der Wandelsterne weltenweisende Mächte.

O Mensch, erwese dich durch den Weltenkreis !

FROMMSEIN O Mensch, erhalte dir in deines Geistes Schaffen
Der Ruhesterne himmelkündende Worte.

O Mensch, erschaffe dich durch die Himmelsweisheit !

VERSE for Lesson 9, part A

Life

Earth
O human being, inwardly sense in your body's entire being,   1
how for you, in existence, earthly-powers are supports.   2

Water
O human being, experience in the entire sphere of your sensing-
feeling,   3
how for you, in existence, water-beings are shapers.

Air
O human being, sense faintly within, in your life's entire living
fabric, how for you, in existence, airy-powers are nurturers.   4,5

Fire
O human being, give thought as to how, in the entire flow of   6
your awareness,   7
for you, in existence, powers of fire are helpers.   8

O human being, perceive yourself in the realm of the elements !

Love

O human being, thus let be active in the depths of your soul
the Earth-guiding planetary Powers.   9

O human being, take on being through the encircling cosmic sphere !

Piety

O human being, preserve for yourself, in the creative activity of
your mind,   10
the heaven-proclaiming words of the stars.

O human being, create yourself through the wisdom of the heavens !

COMMENTARY: VERSE for Lesson 9, part A

Core lesson: Try to realize, existentially, how significant are the elemental beings for the human being who is existing in a physical-etheric body. But these are influences which lose their importance once a body-free higher consciousness is attained.

1 "inwardly sense": the phrases used in the usual versions, 'touch and perceive', or 'sense out', or 'touch and sense' are not helpful. The German verb ('ertasten') has the meaning of detecting with the mind or soul through making some effort; so an **inner** sensing. This rare verb refers to the soul making the effort to register or detect something, whereas usually, the verb 'tasten' is used, which simply means to sense or touch something. Here is an example of Rudolf Steiner using this rare verb, 'ertasten' :

> "Dies zweifache Fähigkeit, die Farbe als Bewegung zu empfinden, to ertasten, gleichsam zu hören..." (GA 291a, p.377)

= "this twofold capacity, to experience the colour, to inwardly sense it, to 'hear it', so to speak"

2 "how for you, in existence": this unusual and repeated word-order is important here. It points out something which occurs for us, in that we are incarnate; "earthly powers" refers to the activity of the gnomes.

3: "sensing-feeling": the translations here usually have 'touching' and the German word often means this, but here it seems that sensing by the soul, of the world outside of our body, is meant. So, a kind of an 'inner touching' rather than the skin's capacity for sensory awareness. Such awareness may often be transmitted by the skin, but it is more than that, for the undines and water-ether determine our contours, the periphery of our face, and body in general. So it is about the interface of our body and the environs, as felt or sensed by our soul; "water-beings" refers to the activity of the undines.

4 "faintly sense inwardly": the usual translation, 'feel and perceive', is not accurate, for here is that special verb, which we noted in detail in the Prelude Verse, and means an inner vague or dim sensing-feeling-awareness. The term, "airy powers", refers to the sylphs.

5 "life's entire living fabric": usually translated as 'life's weaving'; but the term 'weaving' is at times wrongly used in anthroposophical literature. For often what is meant in a text, is not a metaphorical weaving, but a living-ness, an active-beingness. Here the term 'weaving' appears to be less correct than the more subtle and very appropriate other meaning of this verb: 'active living-ness'. This is how Martin Luther used it, for example:

> "....Christum in uns lassen leben, <u>weben</u>" = "...bring it about, that in us Christ lives,
> **is livingly-actively present;**   [not to have Christ 'weaving' in us].

So, here 'weben' is better rendered in English, where the dynamics within the etheric-astral auras are the focus, not as an action (weaving) but more as a noun: 'life's entire living fabric'.

6 "give thought as to": the German word (erdenken) is usually translated as 'think and perceive', which is reasonably accurate; although the 'perceive' aspect is in the background of this rare word. It means, more precisely, to think out, think about, invent or imagine, by some inner effort.

7 "awareness": the German here, (Fühlen) very often means 'feeling', and in the usual versions is translated as 'feelings'; but here it means 'awareness' or what you are registering in your consciousness. This meaning was used by Rudolf Steiner, in the "Portal of Initiation" for example, (p.105 and p.89):

"....und mich des Zweifels Stachen fühlen ließ" = *"and which caused me to feel (be aware of) the sting of doubt."*

And also:

"Und fühlen muß ich wie Lebenssaft in mir zerstörend Gift im Andern wird... " = *"and I had to feel (be aware) how the sap of life in me acted as a destructive poison in others."*

8 "powers of fire": (literally, 'fire-mights') this refers to the pyraustas or 'fire sprites'.

Illustration 8, a pastel drawing by Rudolf Steiner, on page 154, may be helpful here.

9 "the Earth-guiding planetary Powers": this section concerns planetary deities (and their associated lesser spirits). Rudolf Steiner in his commentary on this Lesson, refers to these high spirits influencing the Earth through their vibrant, complex, planetary motions around the Earth, affecting the winds and the oceans. He comments that to feel at one with the cosmos as a soul, we need to develop inner rapport with planets (13th Dec. 1924). The translations, "the cosmic powers that guide the planets" and, "the cosmic-guiding powers of the wandering stars" fail to convey this meaning.

10: "creative activity": here the reference is to the creative activity of the intelligence, the mind, which is directly an expression of the stars (of the zodiac); rather than to activity undertaken by our (scarcely developed) 'spirit'. Those versions which include, "retain/maintain in all thy spirit-working..." tend to obscure the meaning.

The use of "wandering stars" and "resting stars" (for ref. 6) is an odd decision, since in English we say 'planets' not 'wandering stars' (which is the German name for the planets, derived from ancient times). Also we say simply 'stars' and not the German expression 'resting stars', which is used to note the difference between the stars and the planets.

Trag' in Denk-Erleben

Das als reinen Sinnen

In der Seele lichtvoll glänzt

Fühlen und Wollen

Und du bist Geist

Unter reinen Geistern.

Trag' in Fühlenskräfte

Die als edle Liebe

Durch die Seele wärmend weben

Denken und Wollen

Und du bist Seele

Im Reich der Geister.

Trag' in Willensmächte

Die als Geistestriebe

Um die Seele wirkend leben

Denken und Fühlen

Und du schaust dich selbst

Als Leib aus Geisteshöhen.

VERSE for Lesson 9, part B

Into the experience of thinking,
which, as pure contemplation
glows, light-filled, in the soul,
carry feeling and will –
and you are *spiritual-intelligence*   1
amongst beings purely of spirit   2

Into feelings' energies
which as noble love
are warmingly active through the soul,
carry thinking and will –
and you are *soul*
in the realm of the spirits   3

Into powers of will existing around the soul   3b
– exerting their efficacy as spiritual impulses -   4,5
carry thinking and feeling:
and you behold *yourself*
as body, from spiritual heights   6

COMMENTARY: VERSE for Lesson 9, part B

Core lesson: Our threefold soul, on a deeper level, has a high spiritual reality behind it.

1 "*spiritual-intelligence*": the German term 'Geist' here is usually translated simply as 'spirit', meaning a spiritual being; in fact one translation has, "a spirit". But there is no article here in German (i.e., it does not say 'the spirit' or 'a spirit'). So the meaning intended is that of 'intelligence' or 'mind', in the higher sense; so "spiritual intelligence" is being referred to, as distinct from the normal earthly consciousness or mind-set.

2 "beings purely of spirit": the German term 'reinen Geistern' here is usually translated in most translations of the verse, as "pure spirits". However, this does not convey the intended meaning, because the meaning is not that such 'pure contemplation' places a person amongst pure, or highly moral, chaste beings, (though they would be of that nature, usually). The adjective 'pure' ('rein' in German) does not only mean 'pure'; here it has its other meanings; namely 'really', 'truly', 'properly', or 'without doubt', or 'in the proper, full sense'. So the mind of the meditant is functioning amidst spirit-beings which have a fully spiritual consciousness; that is, free of earthly, brain-bound ways of thinking. In other words, in the state of body-free 'thinking' i.e., attaining Psychic-Image onsciousness (or 'Imagination'), the successful meditant experiences himself or herself as cognizing in astral thought-forms, amongst the great numbers of astral beings with similar earth-free, 'cosmic consciousness'.

3 "in the realm of the spirits": it appears that these three states are reflecting the three higher consciousness states. If so, then this verse indicates that something of an initial Cosmic-Spiritual consciousness (or 'Inspiration') is being attained, and one is in the midst of a higher experience. You are a spiritualized soul, now perceiving a glimpse of Devachan.

3b "around the soul": the German text here means in effect, 'in the ambit of' the soul.

4 "exerting their efficacy": the German text here is difficult to put into the English language. It has the word 'wirkend', which we have noted earlier. It is often rendered simply as 'working', but it is better understood as meaning 'exerting its efficacy'; that is, these will-impulses are actively having an influence.

5 "spiritual impulses": this phrase provides a clearer understanding than, "driving-force of the spirit" or "spirit's urges", or "spirit impulses", for in all three sections of the verse, the message is about a somewhat spiritualized person. Hence in their thinking, a higher consciousness exists, and in their feelings, a purified, loving quality is present; and in their will, more ethical or 'spiritual' intentions are now manifesting. So the nuance here is that this person, through her or his own efforts, has developed up to a level where the three soul forces are being spiritualized. The meaning here is not that, from outside of that person, the spiritual world has poured in higher astrality. This dynamic may also be true, but the emphasis here is on the meditant's own efforts and nature; the above alternative translations tend to give more an impression of something happening 'from outside'.

6 "as body": to be beholding oneself as a body, in this last and inherently highest of inner experiences, appears strange at first. But as we consider the progression of inner or clairvoyant experiences in these verses, it becomes clearer what is meant. If a meditant perceives the spiritual reality behind their will, then such a person is cognizing on a Devachanic level; and behind our will is a Devachanic intention, or archetypal Idea, of the body as a vessel of our will.

Notes: The 3 levels of VERSE and lesson 10

Lesson Ten is the first cosmic meditation in the First Class Lessons. My presentation of Lesson Ten is much more comprehensive than is otherwise done. For it is presented in three separate verses. The reason for this is that, in working with this verse, I discovered that although Rudolf Steiner wrote the verse on the blackboard as a complex verse with only a single level in it, the complexity is due to its three levels; three ways of applying it. Three levels are indicated by Rudolf Steiner himself, in his commentary; however he did not especially point this out, but was veiling these deeper levels, as they are not meant for every student of anthroposophy. But for the sake of those ready for these levels, I offer a page for each of these stages, to assist you in using this valuable lesson, on these higher levels. The evidence for such additional stages is provided in the following pages. The reason for the veiled, discreet references to the deeper levels is that they are not intended for those who are new to the path to esoteric development. You need to be cautious here.

The fact of these other levels is confirmed by noting the sparse, but clearly spelt out, commentary by Rudolf Steiner on each of these twelve lines. The numbers to the left indicate the pages where the comments from Rudolf Steiner are found in the German text: 'S' stands for 'page', and three letters tell where on the page these words are to be found; o = above, m = middle, u = below. So, "S23u" means in the lower third of page 23. In the course of the lesson, it is revealed that these 12 lines do refer to two further levels of meaning. It is also the case that there are two separate sequences involved. Level 1 has a particular sequence composed of 3 x 4 lines. Whereas levels 2 & 3 have a different sequence composed of 4 x 3 lines. To try to work with the verse of Lesson Ten in the given sequence of 3 x 4 lines, is not possible, if working with it on levels 2 & 3.

By now the Double and its dangers have been thoroughly noted, and also the meditant is prepared for the inner 'dislocation' of the threefold soul forces and consequently for the assimilation of the cosmic dimensions of these. Now the threshold really opens, and through this Lesson, one can firstly attempt to expand one's ego-sense to include the starry influences. That becoming more aware of the zodiac influences is really important, is confirmed by Rudolf Steiner designing four sets of twelve new images for the zodiac, which indicate the nature of the cosmic influences operative in us over the Ages. (See my book, *The Lost Zodiac of Rudolf Steiner* which presents his previously lost zodiac images.)

But then, secondly, the meditant can go further, to meditate upon his or her existence **prior to conception**. But we can go still further in Level Three, which is intended to assist the meditant to gain insight into **the previous incarnation.** That this is so, is demonstrated by the fact that Rudolf Steiner did specifically refer to these two other levels, in his commentary – but again without emphasizing this. As with the second, deeper meaning of the verse for Lesson One, Rudolf Steiner offers these deeper layers in Lesson 10, discreetly. Consequently, I offer Lesson 10 in **three** pages; these pages guide one as to how to use the verse for these two other levels.

Level One is about the zodiac; it is about the experience of developing an etheric-astral sensing of the stars. Note: the order of the verses in the two other levels is different from that of Level One; for these, it reverts back to a more sequential flow. For Level One, a threefold dynamic is emphasized, involving the 'spiritual depths' (or an insightfulness which is guiding one in meditation), then secondly the feeling response, and then thirdly, that of the will's response. This threefold dynamic, selecting out specific parts of the verse, was only referred to when Level One was being explained, and not when Rudolf Steiner was indicating discreetly the other levels. On these two higher levels, meditating on the 12 lines is undertaken in a different sequence. Illustration 9 shows the great Stuttgart zodiac, from 1912, designed by Rudolf Steiner; its new striking images for each constellation are a meditation on the significance of the zodiac for humanity.

Notes: The 3 levels of VERSE and lesson 10 (cont)

Level Two is about the pre-incarnate phase, or 'pre-conception phase' (abbreviated as 'pcph'). On the page for Level Two, I have entered in smaller fonts, a summary of the words of Rudolf Steiner about what each line now means, regarding the 'pre-conception phase', I give the page number and exact location of his actual words, as found in the German edition of 1977; 'm'= middle of page, 'u' = the lower section of the page, and 'o' = the upper section of the page.

The soul is then in the Moon sphere, where the etheric body shall soon form, as one waits for conception. This level involves a meditative exercise designed to help one attain to a consciousness of one's own soul-life prior to conception, in the moon sphere, existing in one's astral body, (one's newly-formed etheric body will be nearby). The outcome of this meditative exercise is that one remembers one's pre-conception phase, which exists, preserved in the consciousness of one's Guiding Angel, and hence also as an Akashic impression. But we will also perceive our own current responses to this now past phase; and so the comments from Rudolf Steiner move between recalling the past, to the present moment, when a response is felt in the meditative session.

Level Three is a meditation which takes the meditant back into their personality of the previous incarnation; a very significant step in developing higher consciousness. Rudolf Steiner did not provide comments for all 12 lines of the verse in regard to level Three, as he did for Level Two, but he did provide enough indications to confirm this level. I have entered in smaller fonts, a summary of the words of Rudolf Steiner about what each line now means, in regard to the 'previous earth-life phase'.

After the verses, another page of commentary on level 3 clarifies the situation further. It is helpful to note that the words of this verse, having as they do, three levels of meaning, are not always the most appropriate, obvious choice for a line. A sequence of words in a line has to be able to apply to three, quite different meanings; so the meditant has to be flexible, sensing how the word sequence speaks to different meanings.

German text of VERSE for lesson 10

Ich lebe in dem finstren Erdbereich

Sehnend stimmt mich der Erde Finsternis.

Der Erde Finsternis verlöschet mich.

Ich webe in dem Schein der Sterne,

Tröstend ist mir der Sterne Schein,

Der Sterne Schein erwecket mich.

Ich lese in der Geister Taten,

Lehrend sind mir der Geister Taten,

Der Geister Taten rufen mich.

Ich höre in der Götter Sprache,

Schaffend ist mir der Götter Sprache,

Der Götter Sprache zeuget mich.

VERSE for Lesson 10   (level one, the Zodiac)

(When contemplating the stars)

From
depths of
spirit

I'm existing in the dark domain of the Earth

I'm living and moving in the bright light of the stars

I'm reading in the deeds of spirits

I'm hearing in the speech of the gods

The
heart
replies

Yearning arises in me from the Earth's darkness

Comforting to me is the stars' bright light

Instructive to me are the spirits' deeds

Creative to me is the speech of the Gods

The Will
responds

The Earth's darkness extinguishes me

The stars' bright light is awakening me

The spirits' deeds are calling me

The speech of the gods is begetting me

VERSE for Lesson 10 (level two)

The Pre-conception Phase (pcph)

1
S22o

Sp-depth

I'm existing in the dark domain of the Earth

(going back to the moment when the ether-body was being formed)

2
S22m

heart

Yearning arises in me from the Earth's darkness

(a yearning for the spiritual, which also lives in me now, derived from my time in the pcph)

3
S21m

will

The Earth's darkness extinguishes me.

(the Earth does this, to enable the initiatory consciousness which I'm to develop now, in my chamber)

4
S22u

Sp-depth

I'm living and moving amidst the brightness of the stars

(now am back to the pcph, which is to cause an enflamed enthusiastic mood, as an incarnate person)

5
S22u

heart

Comforting to me is the stars' brightness

(a true solace, both in the pcph and also now, in my chamber)

6
S21o

will

The stars' brightness is awakening me

(awakening for me is precisely this perception of, this forging of, a link to the pcph)

7
S23o

Sp-depth

I'm reading in the deeds of spirits

(at the beginning of this incarnation, one was actively existing, moving, amongst these deeds)

8
S23o

heart

Instructive to me are the spirits' deed

(one remembers now, how one was instructed by them in the pcph)

9
S21u

will

The spirit's deeds are calling me

(I notice the spirits calling me, so that their efficacy can beget me in them)

10
S23m

Sp-depth

I'm hearing in the speech of the Gods

(one did indeed hear the Gods in the pcph)

11
S23m

heart

Creative to me is the speech of the Gods

(the speech of the gods is indeed livingly giving birth to me in this pcph)

12
S21u

will

The speech of the Gods is begetting me

(this creative activity about me - it is conceiving me)

VERSE for Lesson 10 (level three)

The Previous Earth-life (pel)

1   Sp-depth   **I'm existing in the dark domain of the Earth**

………...

2   heart   **Yearning arises in me from the Earth's darkness**

……...

3   will   **The Earth's darkness extinguishes me.**

S23u

(one notices that this is occurring in order that one is lead back to the pel:
"I am livingly existing in my previous earthly incarnation".)

4   Sp-depth   **I'm living and moving amidst the brightness of the stars**

……...

5   heart   **Comforting to me is the stars' brightness**

……...

6   will   **The stars' brightness is awakening me**

S24o

(I am placed back into my pel, into what I was then; this is like an awakening)

7   Sp-depth   **I'm reading in the deeds of spirits**

S24m

(I'm now aware of my karmic interconnections, from the Other Side, the realm
of the spirit)

8   heart   **Instructive to me are the spirits' deed**

S23o.24m

(the spirits' activity instructs me as to my karmic interconnected-ness)

9   will   **The spirit's deeds are calling me**

S24m

(I am called upon to fulfill my karma with the spiritual energies which derive
from my pel)

10   Sp-depth   **I'm hearing in the speech of the Gods**

………...

11   heart   **Creative to me is the speech of the Gods**

S24u/25o

(my ego is something which is in the process of continuously coming being !
Illumination occurs as my experience of my pel permeates this present life)

12   will   **The speech of the Gods is begetting me**

S24u/25o

(I have made the journey back to the pel, which now fully permeates this life's
ego; and this, carried out by the gods, makes me into a human being who is
truly in the process of continuously coming into being.)

Commentary: on level 3 of VERSE for Lesson 10

LEVEL THREE

Towards the end of Lesson 10 Rudolf Steiner presents this third level, without any prior notice at all. Level Three involves a much more demanding level, as it unavoidably implies arousing the Double (the most earth-bound impulses in the hidden will energies).

Caution is urged with regard to trying this ! Since it was only discreetly referred to, only those persons who sincerely feel that they have substantially mastered their their lower nature, should attempt to work with this level of the verse.

If, in you, anthroposophy has remained an intellectual achievement, and egoistical traits are not weakened, perhaps even enhanced, these two, semi-veiled, deeper layers are not recommended for you. Indeed none of the First Class Lessons are suitable for students who have not had several years of serious and energetic contemplative study of anthroposophical texts, which have resulted in an ethical re-birth; a commitment to a Christ-centred morality.

For the first half of this third level of usage, one has to work with the lines retrospectively, as it were, to discover that this level exists. For there is no commentary, at this level for lines 1 and 2, but there is a clear commentary for line 3. So, line 3 retrospectively confirms lines 1 and 2 for this level. Likewise, there is no commentary for lines 4 and 5, but there is one, strongly, for line 6.

So the first two segments, each of three lines, are consolidated only towards the end. But for the next segment of three lines – lines 7,8,9 – there is a commentary for each of these lines at this level; but again, the last line is more strongly confirming of this level.

Finally the last segment – lines 10,11,12 – powerfully confirms and upholds the entire fact of Level Three, although this segment has no commentary for its first line.

Note Line 10: **"I'm hearing in the speech of the gods"**; having the word "in", makes this a very unusual phrase, scarcely grammatically possible. For it doesn't say **"listening *to*"** or that one is hearing *something* in (the speech of the gods). It means that the not-yet-conceived soul has a hearing capacity, and this capacity occurs within a special ambient environment – namely the dialogue of divine beings with each other. This is exactly what happens in such an initiatory experience, as briefly revealed by Rudolf Steiner in a comment about sublime beings existing within the streams of light, and one experiences how these beings speak to one from within the light, and how the world had its the origin through this cosmic dialogue, the cosmic Word. This is the actual meaning of the passage in Goethe's fairy tale of *The Green Snake & the Beautiful Lily*, where the golden king receives the answer from the Old Man that "conversation is more quickening than light".

German text of the VERSE for Lesson 11

Ein Welten-Posaunenklang	Welten-Sternen-Stätten, Götter-Heimat-Orte !
Die Seele antwortet	Spricht in Haupteshöhe Menschen-Geistes-Strahlung Das «Ich bin»:
Die Antwort des Angelos	So lebet Ihr im Erdenleibe Als Menschen-Wesenheit.
Ein melodisches Erklingen von den Wandelsternen	Welten-Sonnen-Kreise, Geister-Wirkens-Wege !
Die Seele antwortet	Tönt in Herzensmitte Menschen-Seelen-Weben Das «Ich lebe»:
Die Antwort des Angelos	So schreitet Ihr im Erdenwandel Als Menschen-Schöpferkraft.
Die grollende, raunende Sprache des Weltengrundes	Welten-Grundes-Mächte, Schöpfer-Liebes-Glänzen !
Die Seele antwortet	Schafft in Leibesgliedern Menschen-Wirkens-Strömung Das «Ich will»:
Die Antwort des Angelos	So strebet Ihr im Erdenwerke Als Menschen-Sinnes-Taten.

VERSE for Lesson 11

clarion call of the
cosmic Word
resounds

Starry regions of the cosmos,
dwelling places of gods !

our soul replies

In the head's heights there speaks
radiant glow of human intelligence –   1, 2
    the **'I am'**

our Angel
answers

In this way do ye[*] live in the earthly body   3
as human being.   *(zodiacal deities)

from the solar system
a blissful melodious
resonance resounds

Cosmic en-circlings of the sun,
Pathways of spirits' activity !

our soul replies

In the heart's centre region there resounds
living tapestry of the human soul –
    the **'I live'**

our Angel
answers

In this way do ye[*] stride forth in earthly conduct
as human creative-power.   * (planetary deities)

like rumbling rolling
tones, from the
Earth's crust

Powers of the World-Foundation,   4
radiance of the Creator's love !   5

our soul replies

In the body's limbs is created
currents of human activity –   6
    the **'I will'**

our Angel
answers

In this way ye[*] strive in earthly deeds   7
as human sense-actions.   * (chthonic deities)

Commentary: VERSE for Lesson 11

The verse for this Lesson has been misunderstood in several places. So my translation is very different in several places from the commonly used versions. This verse begins with directing the acolyte's attention up to the zodiac constellations, and hence to where the deities have their abode, whose cosmic intelligence is reflected in our thinking. This situation, of a connection between these zodiacal beings and our consciousness (especially our thinking) is then referred to. The context here is of the human being as placed within a cosmic cross: the Above, the Horizontal and the Lower. So the next line, **"In the head's heights there speaks.."** is pointing out that the head is the uppermost part of us, and corresponds to the upper segment of a cross, and is linked to the starry heights.

The focus of next section is the Horizontal plane, the left and right bars of a cosmic cross, stretching out across the world's circumference, thought of as the horizon which the sun and planets encircle. The heart corresponds in the human being to this middle section of the cosmic cross, so the third line is, *"In the heart's centre region..."* meaning that the heart is a core part of the centre of the human being which corresponds to the horizontal bar of the cosmic cross. It is not referring to **the middle of the heart** but the centre **of the cosmic cross**, and the heart's roughly similar position in the body. The focus of the lower section is on our limbs, and hence the lower, descending bar of the Cosmic Cross, and therefore also the interior of the Earth. The deities which are active behind dense matter and in the Earth's interior are subterranean gods or 'chthonic" deities.

When the short phrase (I am/ I live/ I will) occurs in bold font, this is the soul's way of cognizing and defining the essence of that part of our being; but it is in response to this awareness of the meditant, that our Angel is speaking, indicating the very close intermingling of the macrocosm and the microcosm. That is, the Angel's Spiritual-self consciousness is contemplating the Cosmic Cross and the human soul, wherein cosmic beings are active within human beings.

1 "**human intelligence**": usually translated as the 'human spirit', but here again 'intelligence' appears to be the intended meaning, as our thinking is the focus, and in verse 2, the feelings, and verse 3, the will is the focus.

2 "**radiating glow of**": usually translated as 'radiance' which is also quite correct, but the German word 'Strahlung' (in its rare earlier usage here) has the implication of a dynamically **out-raying glow** - not just a passive glow.

3 "**ye live**": the old form 'ye' is used to indicate that the plural is meant here; namely the divine beings in the zodiac.

4 "**the World-Foundation**": the German term here, "Weltengrund" is a specific term for the Father-God in Theology and also in Anthroposophy, and means 'cosmic-foundation', 'cosmos-fundament', or 'the ground of all being'. So it refers to the Father-God, but in this Lesson it is clear that the sounds derive from the subterranean depths of the Earth. So it points to the Earth's crust and spiritual beings involved in its creation, but also it points to the Father-God, who is the 'fundament' of all Creation. So the term 'world' here is, firstly the Earth, but it also refers to the Father-God's presence 'behind' the mineral crust (the great mountain ranges, etc) of the Earth.

5 "**radiance**": the tones are an expression of the Father-God's love. But Rudolf Steiner informs his audience here, that this love also has a radiance.

6 "**human activity**": literally, efficaciousness, that is, working, creating, being active.

7 "**chthonic**": that is, subterranean deities; beings located inside the Earth.

Commentary: VERSE for Lesson 11   Additional Notes

We noted how, already in Lesson One, Rudolf Steiner discreetly veiled the deeper, more esoteric meanings in the verse, as these are not suitable for every student of anthroposophical wisdom. I have revealed some of these in the course of this book; to do this is always a serious responsibility, and now, in annotating the verse from Lesson Eleven, I again come to the dilemma of how to unveil the deeper implications in this verse. For the outcome of deeper meditation on this verse brings the meditant into direct interface with the underlying purpose of the Class.

On the first level, one learns to acknowledge, and indeed to feel, as something wondrous, that spiritual influences from the zodiac are operative in our thinking, and from the solar system into our general soul-life, and from the Earth's interior into our will (the limbs). We can have a delighted response to Rudolf Steiner' words in this Lesson, "out of what we take up into our heads of the radiance of the stars...there blossoms forth our thinking." He also indicates in other lectures that our intellectual capacity receives its unique qualities from our zodiacal sun-sign, especially GA 151: *Human & Cosmic Thinking.*)

But on a deeper level, these statements open up the potent, burningly relevant question: what am I? If a zodiacal influence, say Leo, underlies my current thinking and attitudes, and in the next life it may be Libra, where am "I" in all this? What am I? If my current "I" identifies with Leo – all my ways of thinking, assessing, intellectually reacting are Leonine – what is there of myself in this, since in a future life it may be Libra. Since in this verse, my Angel is stating that my current Leo sense of "I" is derived from zodiacal gods, a more potent push can hardly be encountered towards asking, where is there a real, an eternal "I" which is somehow "me". (And equally potent questions arise from the other two sections of the verse; it is just that feelings and will are not directly experienced as "I".) The answer, in a general sense, is that upon achieving the Spiritual-self, an eternal, all-encompassing "I" is experienced, and the many questions that this deeper level of the verse creates, become resolved.

A method to work with what is indicated here is to consider spiritual physiology; in particular, the nerve strands in the head. There are actually 12 nerves in our head, referred to as 'cranial nerves'. Rudolf Steiner taught that they are an expression, in matter, of 12 astral streams from the zodiac, raying down into our astral body. He explained that the Hierarchies directed these 12 zodiac streams into the human head, so that the human being would be able to think. (GA 101, 28 Oct. 1907) So if a person's sun-sign is say, Taurus, then we can conclude that the astral stream in the upper part of their aura, which derives from Taurus is radiantly energised, whereas the other astral streams are somewhat dormant. Perhaps also on a subtle level, the 'Taurus cranial nerve' is energised, too.

We can also remind ourselves here that the three influences from the cosmic cross do correlate to the Trinity. The influences "from above", (the zodiac influences) raying into our thinking are an aspect of the Holy Spirit. The influences from the horizontal axis, correlate to the cosmic Christ (the Sun-god), or the Son. The influences rising up from the depths beneath us, correlate to the Father-God, from whose will, Creation, the physical world, came into being. But all three regions of influence are permeated by Luciferic and Ahrimanic energies also.

German text of VERSE for Lesson 12

(Das Weltenwort donnert)

Vernimm des Denkens Feld !

The Guardian speaks:

Es spricht, der dir die Wege
Von Erdensein zu Erdensein
Im Geisteslichte weisen will:

Angel   **Blick' auf deiner Sinne Leuchtewesen.**

Es spricht, der dich zu Seelen
Im stoffbefreiten Seinsgebiete
Auf Seelenschwingen tragen will:

Archangel   **Blick' auf deines Denkens Kräftewirken.**

Es spricht, der unter Geistern
Im erdenfernen Schöpferfelde
Den Daseinsgrund dir geben will:

Archai   **Blick' auf der Erinnerung Bildgestalten.**

(Das Weltenwort donnert)

Vernimm des Fühlens Feld !

The Guardian speaks:

Es spricht, der als Gedanke
Aus Geistes-Sonnenstrahlen
Dich zum Weltendasein ruft:

Exusiai   **Fühl' in deines Atems Lebensregung.**

Es spricht, der Weltendasein
Aus Sternen-Lebenskräften
Dir in Geistesreichen schenket:

Dynameis   **Fühl' in deines Blutes Wellenweben.**

Es spricht, der dir den Geistes-Sinn
In lichten Götter-Höhenreichen
Aus Erdenwollen schaffen will:

Kyriotetes   **Fühl' der Erde mächtig Widerstreben.**

VERSE for Lesson 12

(The cosmic word resounds like thunder)

Perceive the sphere of thinking !

The Guardian speaks:

There speaks one who wants
to show you in spirit light the pathways
from earthly life to earthly life.   1

Angeloi   **Look to the radiant nature of your senses**   2

There speaks one who wants
to carry you on wings of soul
to souls in realms of being freed from matter.

Archangeloi   **Look to the efficacy of your thinking's forces**   3

There speaks one who wants to give you
the basis for existence amongst spirits
in Creator-realms, far from the Earth.

Archai   **Look to remembering's pictorial forms**   4,5

(The cosmic word resounds like thunder)

Perceive the sphere of feeling !

The Guardian speaks:

There speaks one who calls you
to cosmic existence,
as thought, from rays of the Spiritual-Sun.   6

Exusiai   **Feel in your breath's quickening of life**   7

There speaks one who grants you   8
cosmic existence
from life energies of stars, in realms of spirit.

Dynameis   **Feel in your blood's bringing forth of surges**   9

There speaks one who wants to create for you
from earthly will –
in light-filled, lofty realms of gods –
the inner sense for the spirit.   10

Kyriotetes   **Feel the Earth's mighty resistance !**   11

Commentary: VERSE for Lesson 12

Core lesson: To summarize this Lesson is not useful; it has a great deal of esoteric implications which are left unexplained in Rudolf Steiner's commentary – left for the meditant to gradually intuit.

Many of the verses in Lessons 12 and 13 include the admonition from a spiritual being to "Look to...." This means the same as 'consider' or 'observe' or 'give attention to'. But Rudolf Steiner has not used these verbs, instead the phrase, 'look to' or 'look upon', (in German, 'blick auf') which emphasizes the visual quality of a higher thinking, in effect a more enlivened, almost clairvoyant perceiving.
Note: the Guardian twice says "perceive the field of ...", the German verb can mean 'listen' but here it means to 'listen with the soul', so I have chosen 'perceive' to convey this.

1 "in spirit light": in astral imagery, formed of astral light, the Angel wishes to reveal our previous lifetimes; the main focus of this line is not that the pathways themselves, from life to life, proceed along in astral light.

2 The Angel now says, *"Look to the radiant nature of your senses"* as guidance for the serious esoteric meditant in the quest to perceive her or his past lives, and to thus gain karmic awareness, because all sensory impressions are carried in the ether, and mediated to our awareness via our etheric body. If the ethers were not involved, there would be no sensory impressions received. For example, hearing a sound invokes the tone-ether, and this ether, like all the ethers, has its own radiance. When a person becomes especially sensitive to sensory impressions, then the etheric energies, the radiant ether force mediating the sense impressions, is perceived. This beginning of a clairvoyant capacity is required for those to whom some images of their past life are being granted by the Angel, because such astral scenes are absorbed into one's etheric body and then conveyed to the soul.

3 The Archangel now says, *"Look to the efficacy (effects) of your thinking's forces"*, as a help for the meditant in becoming able to consciously function in the astral realm, and thereby commune with other souls. This is said because the meditant, seeking access to the astral realms needs to be aware of what is the impact in their etheric body of their inner life, in particular, their ideation, and also of ideas which then have an existence in the astral body. Ideation or the process of forming mental images, results in these images existing in the etheric body, from whence they exert an influence upon the astral body. Mental images and the more substantial thought-forms which we call 'ideas', which are derived from a subtle materialism or egotism, or which embody unpleasant, negative qualities, continuously radiate out these 'messages' into the soul. It is the effect of these images stored in the etheric body, their 'messages', which form the primary feature of anthroposophical psychology. The more spiritually aligned are one's thoughts, that is, the more one has attained to a conceptual grasp of higher truths, or even to experiencing spiritual insights, which by-pass the brain's logical processes - but which can be expressed to some extent in conceptual form - the more enabled is the meditant to cognize in non-earthly spheres.

4 "memory's pictorial forms": in the common translation "...your memory" but the German is more accurately rendered simply as 'memory' or 'the memory', because, although earlier it was 'your thinking" and "your sensing" in German, it is here simply "memory's pictorial forms".

5 The Principality now says, *"Look to Remembering's pictorial forms"*, as a foundation for existence in spiritual worlds. We need to recall now that the person who is seeking to be self-

Commentary: VERSE for Lesson 12, page 2

conscious, to have an "I" in the astral realms, needs to be aware of their memories, for as Rudolf Steiner explains, these form the actual basis of the sense of "I", both when we awaken each morning, and when we awaken in the spiritual world after death.

6 "....thought, from rays of the Spiritual-Sun" : at first this is an unusual, stark thought. It is first found in a lecture from Aug. 1904: "We humans, seen from a higher plane, are, in the first instance, thoughts of the Cosmos-Spirit, thoughts which have been cast into a form." As explained in my *The Foundation Stone Meditation - a New Commentary*, the phrase, 'the Cosmos-Spirit', was used by Rudolf Steiner in several quite specific ways. Here it means the highest of the Powers or Exousiai, that is, the great sun-god, the cosmic Christ.

7 The Sun-god (the highest of the Powers), **"Feel in your breath's quickening of life"**. The underlying reason for these words is indicated in the Book of Genesis (2:2-7):

> Ge 2:2 By the seventh day, God (here, the Elohim { אֱלֹהִים } had finished
> the work he (they) been doing; so on the seventh day he (they) had
> rested from all his (their) work.
> Ge 2:3 And God [i.e., the Elohim] blessed the seventh day and made it
> holy, because on it he (they) rested from all the work of creating that he
> (they) had done.
> Ge 2:4 This is the account of the heavens and the earth when they were
> created. When the LORD God (here, it is Jehovah { יְהֹוָה } made the earth
> and the heavens —
> Ge 2:5 and no shrub of the field had yet appeared on the earth and no
> plant of the field had yet sprung up, for the LORD God (Jehovah) had not
> sent rain on the earth and there was no man to work the ground,
> Ge 2:6 but streams came up from the earth and watered the whole surface
> of the ground—
> Ge 2:7 the LORD God (Jehovah) formed the man from the dust of the
> ground and breathed into his nostrils the breath of life, and the man
> became a living being.

We note first, verse 7: "the LORD God (this is in Hebrew, 'Jehovah') breathed into Adam, and he became a living soul": that is, in Lemurian times humanity progressed up from primitive amphibian creatures to air-breathing beings. This process was inaugurated and guided by the sun gods, and finalized with the specific help of Jehovah, whose influence is exerted from the moon sphere. That there is an over-arching solar influence behind Jehovah, is indicated in Genesis by referring firstly to the sun-gods (this is, in Hebrew, the 'Elohim') in verses 2 and 3, and only then referring to Jehovah, in verses 5 and 7. So this 'coming alive' of primordial human beings was intertwined with the solar gods: and their relationship to us is expressed in the great rhythm of the sun as it moves around the zodiac. The sun, as experienced from the Earth, moves around the zodiac over 25,920 years; this involves a living interaction with the Earth and humanity. Our breathing, through which we interact with our environs, has the same rhythm as that of the sun, but on a vastly smaller scale: we take 25,920 breaths each day.

8 "grants you": not "would grant", nor "fain would grant..." as given in the official book of these lessons from Dornach. (Technically, the translators for that book misread "schenket" as a subjunctive case, (but if so, it would be a 2nd person plural); it is actually an archaic poetic verbal form of the 3rd person singular indicative case.

Note: We mentioned (p.38) that some errors still exist in the German text; here the Greek spelling of the plural of 'Dynamis' is incorrect, it is in the singular, it should be 'Dynameis'. So I have corrected this word for the German verse accordingly.

9 The Dynameis say, **"Feel in your blood's bringing forth of surges"**: here the common translations have 'wave-weaving', but this does not really convey the meaning of the German term (Wellenweben), which refers to an inherent, mysterious feature of our blood stream: the impulse **to rhythmically surge**. The German word 'Wellen' also means a 'surge', not only a 'wave', and also 'weben' often means 'to produce', in the sense of 'bring forth'. It is precisely this inner quality in the blood stream, to which the meditant should direct her or his attention. In medical lectures, Rudolf Steiner had the courage to reveal that the heart does not pump the blood, although it assists its circulation. But rather the blood has its own inner inherent capacity to circulate – derived from the astral and etheric forces present 'behind' the physical blood. This inner capacity is connected to the high divine beings, from the Mars sphere, the Dynameis, the Mights, or Spirits of Movement. Indeed their name derives from their capacity to bring the planets in our solar system into motion. And also, as a result, their influence bestows on our bloodstream the capacity for movement (lect. 19. Nov. 1911).

10 **"the inner sense for the spirit"**: this term means a mindset for, or an inner resonance with, the spiritual. One could also say, "the attuning of your mind to the spirit"; for this means the intuitive soul-state, which we can experience through our spiritual-soul (or consciousness-soul), and which the Spiritual-self fully has. So the German phrase, when expanded, means "intuitive spiritual consciousness". With this verse, we are in the Jupiter sphere, the realm of the Spirits of Wisdom, and our spiritual-soul in fact derives from being open to influences from this sphere, (this is taught by Rudolf Steiner for example, in GA 231, lect.17-11-1923).

11 **"Feel the Earth's mighty resistance"**: the fallen Luciferic and Ahrimanic forces active in the etheric and astral realms of our planet, in the Earth-sphere oppose any influences from higher beings that are intended to bring about a spiritual consciousness in human in human beings. Rudolf Steiner has depicted the antagonism of these fallen spirits in the Earth-sphere to any efforts towards inner freedom (i.e., morality) stirring in the conscious or semi-conscious soul-life. This dynamic is shown in the north **Green Window of the Goetheanum**, see illustration 10. The verse informs us that the Earth develops a mighty 'resistance' to the spiritual, and the caption for this green window tells us that, "The Spirit of Heaviness gathered the Opposition, and there developed Resistance in the human will".

To engage with this verse meditatively, we need to notice how there are ascending levels of consciousness involved in the second part of the verse for this Lesson. It starts with the sun-gods, the Spirits of Form, trying to awaken the meditant into awareness that he is a thought conceived by these deities. Then it moves up to the Mights or Spirits of Movement, who strive to endow the meditant with some pulsing, vibrant life. Now in this last section, the Dominions are seeking to bestow some actual intuitive-spiritual consciousness, which is a Devachanic awareness. But this high self-awareness is now that of a non-corporeal being existing in spiritual worlds; not as someone whose awareness is is in fact defined by the physical body, at least in part.

If 'spiritual will' means having a spiritual-intuitive awareness, capable of functioning in spiritual worlds, then in contrast to this, 'earthly will' means those intentions which are focussed on practical earthly concerns, and dictated by sensory perceptions, as well as lowly desires and even criminal impulses: these last two are actually astral urges, and not really 'will' in the true sense, but which are regarded in everyday life as part of the will. We noted this with the verse for Lesson One, "*Where sentient beings, powerful in will*, is really saying, *Where resolutely, Beings...*" The task of the Dominions is to help the human being transform this shadowy, partly malignant force into the Spiritual-self, where a nobleness in the quality can blossom, removing the veiled anti-social urges. This goodness in the will is called 'moral intuition' by Rudolf Steiner in his *Philosophy of Freedom*. This is the capacity for the will to be thoroughly ethical, creating a kind, loving good-will, as the essence of one's volition.

The Spiritual-self brings of course, clairvoyant faculties; the self is able to cognize, to consciously perceive, in spiritual realms. As the book *An Outline of Esoteric Science* describes, our capacity to respond to our environs at all, first arose in the 7th cycle of the Sun Aeon, through the continuous interweaving of influences from the Dominions. Through this, a delicate, preliminary form of sentiency arose. The Spiritual-self arises as the astral body, especially the sentient–soul, is purified, for this is the foundational element of our astral nature, our soul-life. That the Dominions are especially mentioned in this verse with regard to developing "an inner sense for" or an awareness of, the spirit, may be due to their pivotal involvement in our soul-life since remote Ages. It was in the first cycle of the Sun Aeon that these great beings developed in humanity a sentiency, a capacity to sense to our environs, and now, in our times, they are attempting to develop in us the capacity to sense, to cognize, non-sensory, spiritual environs.

German text of VERSE for Lesson 13

Das Weltenwort donnert

Vernimm des Willens Feld !

der Hüter der Schwelle:

Es spricht, der die Weltenkräfte, die dumpfen

Aus den Erden-Untergründen, den finstren

In deiner Glieder Regsamkeiten lenket:

Throne   *Blick' auf deiner Triebe Feuer-Wesen.*

Es spricht, der die Geistesstrahlen, die hellen

Aus Gottes-Wirkensfeldern, gnadevoll

In deinem Blute kreisen läßt:

Cherubine   *Blick' auf des Gewissens Seelen-Führung.*

Es spricht, der das Menschensein – das vollbrachte –

Durch Tode und Geburten, sinngerecht

Zum Atmen bringt in gegenwärt'ger Zeit:

Seraphine   *Blick' auf deines Schicksales Geistes-Prüfung.*

VERSE for Lesson 13

(The cosmic word resounds, like thunder)

Perceive the field of Will !

The Guardian speaks:

There speaks one who guides cosmic forces
muffled, deep tones –   1
from subterranean depths of the Earth
the darkly obscured –   2
into the lively energy of your limbs.   3

Thrones   **Look to the fire-nature of your impulses**   4

There speaks one who,
as an act of Grace,
from God's realms of activity
brings to circulation in your blood
the rays of the Spirit –
the brightly shining.

Cherubine   **Look to the soul-guiding of the conscience**

There speaks one who in current times,
brings human existence
– the achieved –   5
through deaths and births
to breathe again,   (*to vitality of expression*)   6
according to its actual nature.   7

Seraphine   **Look to the spiritual trials of your destiny**

Commentary: VERSE for Lesson 13, page 1

Note: The German verse has the word for the Thrones in the plural, in German, not in the ancient Greek plural. This also occurs in Lesson 15, even though the names of all of the divine beings below the Thrones, are given in Greek.

1 "muffled, deep tones": when this verse is rightly understood, this phrase (*die dumpfen*) joins with "the darkly obscured" (*den finstren*) to create a superbly poetic quality; each adjectival phrase intensely defines the noun it refers to. 'Dumpfen' can have the meaning of sounds that are muffled or dull (and often deep) and was used by Rudolf Steiner in exactly this way, e.g., "...die Wirkung des dumpfen Lautes": "the effect of muffled-dull sounds (of speech)" in GA 276a p.149. He also refers to just such deeper, rumbling subterranean tones in Lesson 11.

2 "the darkly obscured": not 'dark immensity' nor 'darkest depths'. The word has the nuance of 'dark' and of 'obscured'; and here both meanings are meant. This verse in general is about the will-forces operative in the human being, which are deeply veiled; being partly evil, partly highly spiritual. These forces are originally from the Thrones (the highest of whom is the Father-God, in an initial sense), which also brought forth the mineral physical layers of the planet. But these energies are shrouded in a darkened malignant astrality from Ahrimanic powers in the Earth's interior, and hence also in the lower urges of the human being.

3 "lively energy": the German word here, "Regsamkeiten", if translated literally, is the 'liveliness-es' of the limbs.

4 "Look upon the fire-nature of your impulses": it was in the Saturn Aeon that the Thrones emanated forth the high Devachanic energies which became the underlying basis of our physical body and the Earth. As the Earth condensed and humanity drew down into the material realm, Ahriman and Lucifer could exert their influence, and from this, evil came into being. So, a malignant burning inner fire arose, enflamed by sensual desires and aggressive urges. But there are also noble, moral will-energies too.

5 "The achieved": the German word here means 'the accomplished/achieved", but as Rudolf Steiner's commentary explains, it refers to human existence, up to the stage that it has evolved, so far. These Seraphine have accomplished some of their goals. What they are doing now is based on what been accomplished so far, from the past.

Note:
This third verse has two idiomatic phrases, so it has several possible meanings, because idioms can be understood in several ways.

7 We explore this idiom first, although in German it comes second. Idiom 1"**sinngerecht**": in the common versions it is translated as "meaningful justice". It is just possible that here Rudolf Steiner has used it in this way. But this German word has never meant that; but rather, '*appropriate to (according to) the true meaning (of something)*: *i.e.*, in modern terms, according to *its 'own truth', its own reality*. In the common versions with an unusual view of 'sinngerecht' as "meaningful justice", the verse is saying the Seraphine's actions in regard to integrating humanity's past into its current karma, are carried out *with justice*: and their influence lives on and pulses within the 'form' of our breathing. One translation has in fact even merged 'breathing' with the Seraphinic 'justice', to say: "*brings human existence....rightfully (justly) to breathe*".

But using the proper meaning of this idiom, the verse is saying, the Seraphine's actions regarding integrating humanity's past into its current karma, are in accordance with the human being's *actual meaning or purpose*, and this lives and pulses in the 'form' of our breathing. Therefore we shall now consider this verse again:

Commentary: VERSE for Lesson 13, page 2

> There speaks one who in current times,
> brings human existence –
> the achieved,
> through deaths and births –
> to breathe again,
> **according to its actual nature**.   (or, 'with meaningful justice' ?)

It's very unlikely Rudolf Steiner used 'sinngerecht' here to mean 'meaningful justice'. It seems to me that a more correct translation is 'according to its true meaning' or 'its actual nature'. We note that the proper meaning of this idiom offers a deeper message.

6 Idiom 2 "**zum Atmen bringen**": this is translated as "**to breathe again**" and this is indeed one of its meanings, especially in medical circumstances, where it means to get someone to breathe. So, taken as meaning **to breathe again**; it is saying "the Seraphine's actions regarding humanity, bring us to breathing again (when back into earthly life). This is confirmed by Rudolf Steiner's very brief commentary on this verse, where he does refer to breathing, saying in effect that its "form" arises from all of humanity's evolutionary journey during previous lifetimes so far.

Using this version, as we need to, following Rudolf Steiner's commentary, we perceive the message that the Seraphine bring people down to physical life and hence breathing – and in some way, not perceived by us, nor explained in the Lesson, our past has led to a destiny in contemporary times which is manifested in the 'form' of our breathing.

But this phrase "zum Atmen bringen", is a common idiom which means, "to give a **vitality of expression** to / give 'real' life to / give a living vitality to / or metaphorically 'bring to life'. If the verse is translated in this second way, thought of as a second meaning, subtly present behind the main meaning of "to breathe again", then this gives rise to another deep message, one which is still supportive of the usual primary interpretation.

> There speaks one who in current times, brings human existence – thus far achieved, through deaths and births – *into vitality of expression*, according to its* actual nature (or, real meaning).   (* humanity's)

But now the verse gains this important secondary message: "the Seraphine's actions regarding humanity's past lifetimes are offering us a real *vitality of expression* as we incarnate by the integration of our karma, such as the choice of year and nation, and family, etc." Their action creates the best opportunities for a person's development. This alternative version, like the usual interpretation, conveys a valid truth. It is likely that this is meant to be included, leading the meditant to another perspective on the words from the Seraphine, "Look upon the spirit-testing of your destiny". The meditant can then contemplate this admonition from a Seraphim as part of such an alternative version. That is, we can contemplate our incarnation as a vitalized, enhanced reality, which is in harmony with our inner meaning and purpose.

We can discern a profound meaning in the trial and tribulations, in the gifts and opportunities, that our life offers us, precisely through its timing, and placement (in terms of the national and familial context of our life). This is a meditative exercise which has potent meaning. By contrast, to contemplate the admonition from a Seraphim, "Look to the spirit-testing or our destiny" within the usual translation of the verse, "**to breathe again**" means that Seraphinic influence is a force which is imperceptibly influencing and forming the nature of our breathing. This is a much more elusive idea to contemplate.

Spiritual sign-post or 'tablet'

The following verse was also given in this Lesson. It is referred to as a (spiritual) 'tablet' seen in the spiritual worlds, (alluding to the tablets of stone that Moses brought down from the mountain, with the 10 Commandments)

I entered into this sense world

bringing with me the legacy of thinking.   1

A divine power has led me here.

Death, it stands the end of the way.

I want to feel the Christ-being.

This awakens, in death of matter, spirit-birth.

Thus in spirit do I find the world,

and know myself in cosmic evolving.

German text of the verse

Ich trat in diese Sinnes-Welt

Des Denkens Erbe mit mir führend,

Eines Gottes Kraft hat mich hereingeführt.

Der Tod, er steht an des Weges Ende.

Ich will des Christus Wesen fühlen.

Es weckt in Stoffes-Sterben Geist-Geburt.

Im Geiste find' ich so die Welt

Und erkenne mich im Weltenwerden.

1 **"legacy"**: whereas we may think of a legacy as something positive, a kind of gift to a later generation, from someone, or from a group of people who have died, here it has a negative meaning. It is pointing to the dying away of the spiritual cosmic consciousness, which we had in spiritual worlds, as we descend into the body. Here on Earth, using the brain to be aware of our thoughts, we have an intelligence, our intellectual logical mind, which is a vague, hollowed-out form of consciousness, compared to spiritual consciousness. It is in the developing of the Spiritual-self by meditation, that this higher spiritual consciousness awakens, and this is a process which the Christ-light, absorbed into one's aura, makes possible.

German text of VERSE for Lesson 14

Hüter: Wo ist der Erde Festigkeit, die dich stützte?

Christus: Ich verlasse ihren Grund, so lang der Geist mich trägt.

Lucifer: Ich fühle wonnig, daß ich fortan der Stütze nicht bedarf.

Ahriman: Ich will durch Geistes Kraft fester noch sie hämmern.

Hüter: Wo ist des Wassers Bildekraft, die dich durchdrang ?

Christus: Mein Leben verlöscht sie, so lang der Geist mich formt.

Lucifer: Mein Leben zerschmilzt sie, daß ich erlöst von ihr werde.

Ahriman: Mein Leben befestigt sie, daß ich sie ins Geistgebiet versetze.

Hüter: Wo ist der Lüfte Reizgewalt, die dich erweckte?

Christus: Meine Seele atmet Himmelsluft, so lang der Geist um mich
        besteht.

Lucifer: Meine Seele achtet ihrer nicht in Geistes Seligkeit.

Ahriman: Meine Seele saugt sie auf, daß ich göttlich schaffen lerne.

Hüter: Wo ist des Feuers Reinigung, die dir das Ich erflammte?

Christus: Mein Ich lodert im Gottesfeuer, so lang der Geist mich
        zündet.

Lucifer: Mein Ich hat Flammenmacht durch Geistes Sonnenkraft.

Ahriman: Mein Ich hat Eigenfeuer, das rein durch Selbstentfaltung
        flammt.

VERSE for Lesson 14

Guardian: Where is the Earth's solidity that supported you ?

Christ: I relinquish its basis, so long as the spirit sustains me.

Lucifer: I feel blissful, that from now on, I have no need of the supports.

Ahriman: I want to hammer it even denser through the spirit's power.

Guardian: Where is the water's forming power which permeated you?

Christ: My existence extinguishes this, so long as the spirit forms me.

Lucifer: My existence dissolves this, that I may be released from it.

Ahriman: My existence strengthens this, that I may transfer it into the spirit realm.

Guardian: Where is the inciting, stimulating power of the wind, which awakened you?

Christ: My soul breathes heaven's air, so long as the spirit remains around me.

Lucifer: My soul disregards it in blissfulness of spirit.

Ahriman: My soul draws it in, that I may learn to create as the gods do.

Guardian: Where is the fire's cleansing, which enflamed the I for you?

Christ: My I blazes in God's fire, so long as the spirit enkindles me.

Lucifer: My I has the power of flames through the spirit's solar force. 1

Ahriman: My I has its own fire, which flames solely through self-unfolding.

Commentary: VERSE for Lesson 14

Core Lesson: This verse concerns the attitude which we need to have regarding the four elements that form and sustain our personality. This advice is needed even though, in a meditative state we are functioning in a spiritual state, disconnected from our sensory, bodily existence.

There are three important underlying purposes here. One is that it keeps the meditant aware of the contrast between their earthly, physical-etheric nature, and their soul-spiritual nature. Secondly, it teaches that the four elements, and their four associated ethers, play a potent role in maintaining our personality, and that supportive influences must be present, to provide similar, alternative support for our soul, our consciousness, when we are not in a bodily state.

Thirdly, we are made aware that once we are functioning in the astral realm, we have to specifically, actively, choose a wholesome mode of maintaining our soul. We have to choose the equivalent of an underlying earthly 'solidity'; this is to allow the higher, divine being-ness to provide the basis to our being; no longer the life-ether, activated by gnomes. Thus a Luciferic or Ahrimanic influence to this part of our earthly being is excluded.

We also have to rise above the forming, sculpting influence of the tone-ether (or water-ether) activated by undines. In this way, the higher astral influences themselves are felt to be forming a boundary and contours of my "I" sense. Again a Luciferic or Ahrimanic influence to this part of our earthly being is excluded.

Note: The phrase **"my existence"** replaces the translation "my life" of the usual translations, because this latter phrase, when properly used, actually refers to being alive on the Earth, and not to functioning in spiritual worlds. This more precise use of language is not hairsplitting; it is an attempt to correct a very widespread lack of clarity in the use of the word 'life'. The word 'life' in German ('Leben') does not only mean 'life', it also means 'existence, existing'. When meditating upon this verse, the distinction is very important.

In addition, the liveliness and alertness of the feelings, of the soul in general, has to be experienced as derived from the higher astral being-ness of the spiritual world; no longer from the light-ether, activated by sylphs. And as with the other two ethers, a Luciferic or Ahrimanic aspect to this part of our earthly being is to be excluded.

Finally, the role of the warmth-ether, with its pyraustas (or 'fire-elementals'), from which the sense of "I" derives a strong impetus, has to be replaced by a capacity to experience the 'fire' of the divine being-ness of the higher astral realm. The Luciferic temptation, to be 'fired up' in bliss with a kind of counterfeit solar fire, is to be avoided; that is, a fire force which comes from Lucifer, whose realm is very near to, but is not actually a true part of, the sun sphere. Likewise the sinister, coldly-burning fire which Ahriman has, and eventually which suggests attaining the power to dominate over other souls, needs to be resisted.

1 **"spirit's solar force"**: this phrase is accurate to the German, whereas the translation in the usual versions, "power of the spiritual sun", is not correct. The significant point here is that Luciferic attitudes are speaking, and although Lucifer would like to present his realm as part of the Spiritual-sun and to convince human beings that this is the situation, this is false. His light is a counterfeit of true solar light, and as such, it appeals to self-centred, indulgent. attitudes. So the German text avoids saying "the spiritual-sun", instead offers a vague phrase which can give that impression, perhaps even intends to give that impression, but does not actually say this.

Note that the next verse, no. 15, takes this meditative lesson into its higher conclusion, and adds specific details: namely how the divine-spiritual beings of the Hierarchies provide a substitute for these earthly elemental influences.

The German text of VERSE for Lesson 15

Der Hüter: Was wird aus der Erde Festigkeit, die dich stützte?
(Aus der dritten Hiertarchie antworten...)

Die Angeloi:
Empfinde, wie wir in deinem Denken empfinden.

Die Archangeloi:
Erlebe, wie wir in deinem Fühlen erleben.

Die Archai:
Schaue, wie wir in deinem Wollen schauen.

Der Hüter spricht:
Was wird aus des Wassers Bildekraft, die dich durchdrang?
(Aus der zweiten Hierarchie antworten...)

Die Exusiai :
Erkenne Geistes-Welten-Schaffen im Menschen-Körper-Schaffen.

Die Dynameis :
Erfühle Geistes-Welten-Leben im Menschen-Körper-Leben.

Die Kyriotetes :
Wolle Geistes-Welt-Geschehen im Menschen-Körper-Sein.

Der Hüter spricht:
Was wird aus der Lüfte Reizgewalt, die dich erweckte?
(Aus der ersten Hierarchie antworten...)

Die Throne:
Ergreife wissend Innen-Sein in deinem Gottes-Welten-Sein.

Die Cherubine :
Erwarme am Innen-Leben in deinem Gottes-Welten-Leben.

Die Seraphine :
Erweck' in dir Innen-Licht in deinem Gottes-Welten-Licht.

VERSE for Lesson 15

Guardian: What becomes of the Earth's solidity that supported you?
(beings from the 3rd hierarchy speak; there resounds from the darkness)

Angeloi: Perceive how we are perceiving in your thinking.   1

Archangeloi: Experience how we are experiencing in your feeling.

Archai: Behold how we are beholding within your willing.   1b

Guardian: What becomes of the water's forming power which permeated you?
(beings from the 2nd hierarchy speak; there resounds from the darkness)

Exusiai: Cognize spirit realms' creating, in the human body's
         creating.   2

Dynameis: Faintly within feel spirit realms' existence, in the human
           body's existence   3

Kyriotetes: Will spirit world's occurrences, in the human body's
            being.   4, 5

Guardian: What becomes of the inciting-stimulating power of the winds, which awakened you?
(beings from the 1st hierarchy speak; there resounds from the darkness)

Thrones: With cognizance take hold of inner being, in your divine
            cosmic being.   6

Cherubim: Enkindle warmth of inner existence, in your divine
           cosmic existence.   7

Seraphim: Awaken inner light in you, in your divine cosmic light.

Commentary: VERSE for Lesson 15, page 2

Here the Hierarchies speak in the 'imperative mood' in each line; that is, the meditant is urged to achieve what they are suggesting. (Also, the error in the Greek plural for Dynamis has been corrected to, 'Dynameis'.)

1 "**perceive**": the translation here can be either 'perceive' or 'sense', but since 'sense' tends to imply using the sensory organs, yet here one is in the spirit world, I have used 'perceive', to suggest that an 'inner hearing' is meant.

1b "...**beholding within your willing**": the Principalities have a kind of 'inner seeing' into our human reality via our will, that is, via the intuitive consciousness of our volition; this is what underlies our actions. This was known to Hebrew initiates, as shown in Proverbs 20, 27: "The soul of the human being is the lamp of the Lord, shining into his innermost being". Here the Hebrew term Neschamach, is used for 'soul', but it means the intuitive soul-spirit; other Hebrew words for 'soul' refer to the thinking or emotions.

2 "..**human body's creating**": here the word 'creating' is a noun (technically, it is acting as a verbal substantive), and it is ambiguous, meaning either what the body creates, such as all the myriad metabolic processes; or it means the action of divine beings in creating the body. This second meaning is what is meant: I can confirm this from an entry in his private notebook for this verse. It shows that Rudolf Steiner did consider, but then discarded, 'evolving' (and also 'dying'); in vol.4 of the German edition, 1977, p.121.

Special note: the common translations, in having "cosmic spirit-life", etc, are not helpful, for the meaning here is, the spiritual realms and their own 'creating' or their own 'life'. And in the first two lines, spiritual realm<u>s</u> are involved, but in the third line, a single, not a plurality, of spirit is involved; so it is about 'the spirit world'.

3: "**Faintly within feel...**": here, as in the Prelude verse, is that verb which so often is not properly interpreted; it means to faintly, vaguely, or weakly, inwardly sense or feel. So this line means: **try to faintly sense within the life of spirit realms, in your body's life.**

4 "**Will spirit-world occurrences...**": the word, 'will' is here a verb, we need to be aware of this when meditating on this line, but how does one do this? The term, 'the spirit-world' alerts us to cosmic influences on a spiritual level, especially from the planets. In various lectures, Rudolf Steiner refers to the planetary influences in the organs of the trunk of the body (the kidneys, liver, heart, and so on). It appears that the meditant is being urged here to become conscious of this and through this, it is a natural outcome that his or her own will becomes aligned to, and inwardly supportive of, these influences.

5 "**occurrences**": could perhaps be translated as 'process'; but the German word actually means "occurring-ness-es". Lacking such a word in English, a good rendering here is, **occurrences,** meaning, things actively occurring.

Commentary: VERSE for Lesson 15

6 "**Cognizant**": i.e., in a state of enhanced awareness, seek to achieve the realization of the divine reality arising within you, as the Spirit-self forms.

7 "**your divine**...": the last three lines have literally "your godly...." but this word often has an odd or stilted nuance in English.

The German text of VERSE for Lesson 16

Hüter: Was wird aus des Feuers Reinigung, die dir das Ich entflammte?

Angeloi, Exusiai, Thronoi
Erwecke dir in Weltenätherweiten die Lebensflammenschrift.

Archangeloi, Dynameis, Cherubine
Erschaffe dir in Zeitenwellenkreisen die Seelensühnekräfte.

Archai, Kyriotetes, Seraphine
Erbitte dir in ew'gen Wesentaten die Geisterlösermächte.

Der Hüter:
Hat verstanden dein Geist?

Ich:
Der Weltengeist in mir
Er hielt den Atem an
Und seine Gegenwart
Mög' erleuchten mein Ich.

Der Hüter:
Hat begriffen deine Seele?

Ich:
Die Weltenseelen in mir
Sie lebten im Sternenrat
Und ihre Harmonien
Mögen klingend schaffen mein Ich.

Der Hüter:
Hat erlebt dein Leib?

Ich:
Die Weltenkräfte in mir
Sie richten Menschentaten
Und ihre Wahrspruchworte
Mögen lenken mir das Ich. ₁

VERSE for Lesson 16

Guardian: What becomes of the fire's cleansing, which enflamed the I for you?

Angeloi, Exusiai, Thronoi:
Awaken for you, in cosmic ether's wide expanse, the flame-script of life.

1

Archangeloi, Dynameis, Cherubine:
Create for you, in cyclical waves of time, the atonement capacities of the soul.

2

Archai, Kyriotetes, Seraphine:
Entreat for you, in eternal deeds of being, the Spirit's powers of redemption.

3

Guardian: Has your spiritual intelligence understood ?   4

"I": The Spirit of the Cosmos in me,   5
It held its breath –   6
And its presence,
may it illumine mine "I".

Guardian: Has your soul comprehended ?   7

"I": The Souls of the Cosmos in me,   8
They dwelt in the Council of the Stars*   (*the Planets)   9
And their harmonies,
may they, resounding, create mine "I".   10

Guardian: Has your body experienced?   11

"I": The Forces of the Cosmos in me   12
They judge the deeds of the human being –   13
And may their verdict-words guide for me the "I".

Commentary: VERSE for Lesson 16

Note: It is the "I" who answers here, but it is impelled to do this by the hierarchies, thus the response appears to be from the hierarchies, hence it resounds from all sides.
Note: The plural for 'Dynamis' has been corrected (Dynameis).

1 "Awaken for you, in the...": the word order here follows the deliberate word order in the German, which places emphasis upon what the meditant is to do to assist himself or herself.

2 "...in the cyclical waves of time" : rather than 'encircling waves', because the phrase actually means 'the periodically re-occurring time ripples, or time waves'.

3 "Entreat for you, in eternal deeds of being": here within "the eternal deeds of Being", one is not praying for, or to, the Spirit's redeeming might in the usual sense of prayer; but rather one is **entreating** that, within 'the eternal deeds of being' the redeeming-might of the spirit may become manifest in one. So if we regard this inner work as 'praying', it needs to be a mature, wordless, prayerful mood of soul, which arises from within the meditative state.

Note: The guardian now speaks in a more intimate way to the meditant...the "I" responds in a devotional, humble manner.

4 "spiritual intelligence": usually translated as 'Spirit', and this is also correct, but this is often too abstract a term; it means here intelligence as a spiritual faculty, not our earthly logical, intellectuality.

The 3 sections following are about the intelligence, the feeling-sensing capacity, and the will

5 (This section is about intelligence evolving to Spirit-Self) "the Spirit of the Cosmos" in German, 'Weltengeist', this is a special word in Rudolf Steiner's vocabulary, which has several different meanings. A more accurate, but much less poetic translation here is: 'the Cosmic Spiritual-Intelligence'. It can mean the Father God (or hierarchical reflections of Him) or it can mean the Sun-god Christ; or in a more general multi-facetted usage it can mean, as Rudolf Steiner himself explains, what Aristotle called the Nus (or Nous), i.e., cosmic intelligence; this is the cosmic wisdom of the hierarchies, from which our Manas or Spirit-Self derives. It is this third usage which is meant here. It is also associated with the Holy Spirit in the sense of the lower (third) hierarchies.

6 "held its breath": in earlier Ages, as humanity was given intelligence, cosmic wisdom entered into us, and now the 'Spirit of the Cosmos' is awaiting the outcome of this process.

7 (This section is about our sentiency evolving up to Life-Spirit) "comprehended": the German verb has the nuance of understanding, not only by analysing, but by embracing or enveloping with empathy, the words of the Gods.

8 "The Souls of the Cosmos": the beings who constitute the Soul of the Cosmos (its spiritual sentiency and rhythmical dynamics), active in the interaction between stars and planets. It is also associated with the 'Son' or the second group of hierarchies.

9 "Council of the Stars": the word 'Stars' here is unusual; for the planets are what the line refers to, as shown by Rudolf Steiner's commentary. He deliberately uses this vague term, (for in German, one specifies either 'wandering' stars, meaning the planets; or 'resting' stars, meaning the stars of our galaxy).
The ambiguous term 'stars' is used here to imbue 'the planets' with the aura of radiance and power that we usually associate with the actual stars. So the phrase is actually, "the Council of the Planets", that is, Council of the leading Planetary Spirits.

Commentary: VERSE for Lesson 16 (cont)

10 "...Create mine "I": as Rudolf Steiner commented, these words refer to the hope of the meditant regarding forming a higher aspect to their "I"; noble astral influences from the planets are primary qualities of the higher "I". This line is then referring to the process of developing the Spiritual-self.

11 (This section is about the Will, and the influence of the Spirit-human) "your body": not the flesh, but the Will, which manifests via the astral-etheric elemental forces in it.

12 "Forces of the Cosmos": the spiritual energies behind physical creation and our will, associated with the first group, the highest rank of hierarchical beings.

13 "judge the deeds": the karma-decreeing powers of the hierarchies are invoked, that the meditant may intuit the right steps in life in seeking to dissolve ego-centric karmic impulses.

The German text of VERSE for Lesson 17

Der Hüter:

Sieh' des Äther-Farbenbogens
Lichtgewalt'ges Rund,
Lass' durch deiner Augen
Lichterschaffene Kraft
Dein Ich den Kreis durchdringen,
Und dann schau von jenseit'ger Warte
Farbenflutend die Weltenschale.

Angeloi, Archangeloi, Archai:

Empfind' unsrer Gedanken
Farbenatmend Leben
In der Schale Lichtesfluten;
Wir tragen Sinnenschein
In Geistes-Wesensreiche
Und wenden weltdurchdrungen
Uns höhern Geistern dienend zu.

Exusiai, Dynameis, Kyriotetes

Euer Empfangenes
Aus totem Sinnenschein Belebtes:
Wir wecken es im Sein;
Wir schenken es den Strahlen,
Die des Stoffes Nichtigkeit
In des Geistes Wesenheit
Liebewebend offenbaren.

Throne, Cherubine, Seraphine,

In deinen Willenswelten
Fühl' unser Weltenwirken;
Geist erglänzt im Stoffe,
Wenn wir denkend schaffen;
Geist erschafft im Stoffe,
Wenn wir wollend leben;
Welt **ist** Ich-wollend Geisteswort.

VERSE for LESSON 17

The Guardian:

See the intensely radiant arc
of the etheric rain-bow   (colour-bow)   1
Through the light-begotten power of your eyes,
Let your I penetrate the circle,
And then, from yonder vantage point
behold, in cascading colours, the World Chalice.   2,3

Angeloi, Archangeloi, Archai:
(spoken into the human soul)

In the chalice's cascades of light
Feel the colour-breathing life of our thoughts.
We bear sensory semblance
into the spirit's realms of being,
and, permeated by the world,
turn ourselves, in service, to higher spirits.

Exusiai, Dynameis, Kyriotetes:
(spoken to the Angeloi, Archangeloi, Archai)

That which you have received,
and from dead sensory semblance vivified –
we awaken it in being;
we bestow upon it the rays which,
imbued with love, make manifest   4
the voidness of matter in the spirit's being.

Thrones, Cherubine, Seraphine
(spoken to the human soul)

In thy realms of will   5
feel our cosmic efficacy.
Spirit shines in matter
when we, in thinking, create.
Spirit creates in matter
When we, in willing, live.
World **is**: I - willing Spirit-Word

Commentary: VERSE for Lesson 17

Core Lesson: The meditant recalls a physical rainbow, and then the Guardian directs them to contemplate the etheric rainbow, the colours of which are the counter-colours to that of the normal rainbow. Then the meditant imagines going through this etheric colour-arc, up into the firmament and then with astral clairvoyance looking back, and seeing the very large astral form which arises when a rainbow is formed, and which acts as a receptacle to humanity's thought-forms.

Note: the plural for 'Dynamis' has been corrected (Dynameis).

1 "etheric rain-bow": here Rudolf Steiner decided to use the unique term, "colour-bow". This choice may be due to two reasons: the first is, as he commented in 1897, the term 'rainbow' is a poor choice for a phenomenon which is primarily to do with colour, not the rain. Also, it is being seen etherically, so the raindrops are not there, but the colours remain, (although changed).

However, in English the phrase, 'etheric colour-bow' tends to impede feeling for the scene which the Guardian is invoking. The phrase, 'etheric rain-bow' assists the meditant, so richly evocative is the ambience which the word 'rainbow' has in English.

2 "Chalice": the German term 'Schale'can be translated as a cup, vessel, skin, but it also means 'goblet'; hence the word chalice can be chosen, for a chalice is a type of goblet, and it does not have to be restricted to rituals in a church or elsewhere, but it can be used for a receptacle for spiritual energies, rather than for a beverage, etc. The old translation, "Cup o' the World" is especially poorly nuanced.

3 "World": here we encounter again the German term 'Welt', however, its meaning is not so clear. In this Lesson, Rudolf Steiner implies that the etheric form related to any rain-bow is a part of the planet Earth, and yet it is where various cosmic beings are active. Thus it is a part of the Earth (our world), but it is also where spiritual beings, associated with the various planetary spheres, are active; thus it has a cosmic aspect to it as well.

4 "imbued with love": the meaning here is that through the actions of these hierarchical beings, divine Will, which is Love, is actually brought forth, or made actively manifest, for their rays are imbued with the Love. So what the hierarchies have been able to awaken into real meaning from earthly humanity's inner life, is being lovingly taken up.

5 "realms of will": it is in the plural in the German, so our individual will is here described having several facets to it.

German text of VERSE for Lesson 18

Angeloi:
Es denken die Menschenwesen !
Wir brauchen das Licht der Höhen,
Daß wir im Denken leuchten können.

Dynameis:
Empfanget das Licht der Höhen,
Daß ihr im Denken leuchten könnt,
Wenn Menschenwesen denken.

Archangeloi:
Es fühlen die Menschenwesen !
Wir brauchen die Seelenwärme,
Daß wir im Fühlen leben können.

Kyriotetes und Exusiai
Empfanget die Seelenwärme,
Daß ihr im Fühlen leben könnt,
Wenn Menschenwesen fühlen.

Archai:
Es wollen die Menschenwesen !
Wir brauchen die Tiefenkraft,
Daß wir im Wollen wirken können.

Kyritotetes, Dynameis, und Exusiai
Empfanget die Tiefenkraft,
Daß ihr im Wollen wirken könnt,
Wenn Menschenwesen wollen.

VERSE for Lesson 18

Angeloi:
Human beings are thinking !
We need the light of the Heights,
that in the thinking we may shine.

> **Dynameis respond:**
> Receive the light of the Heights
> that ye may shine in the thinking,
> when human beings are thinking.

Archangeloi:
Human beings are feeling !
We need the soul-warmth,
that in the feeling we may live.

> **Kyriotetes und Exousiai respond**
> Receive the soul-warmth,
> that ye may live in the feeling,
> when human beings are feeling.

Archai:
Human beings have will !
We need the power of the Depths,
That in this willing we can be efficacious

> **Kyriotetes, Dynameis, und Exousiai respond**
> Receive the power of the Depths,
> that ye may have efficacy in the willing,
> when human beings are willing.

Commentary: VERSE for Lesson 18

Note: the plural for 'Dynamis' has been corrected (Dynameis).

The verse for this lesson is not as difficult as many of the preceding verses.
In the first section, we learn that a spiritual light is needed by the Angels to uplift the incarnate human being's thinking. The Virtues or Dynameis are the beings who assist the Angels in this. The light flows from the heights; the implication is that this refers to the stars. It's helpful to know that in a discarded preliminary draft of this verse, Rudolf Steiner indicated how important the help of the Dynameis is to the Angels; this draft version states: "*Death threatens human thinking*", instead of just, "*human beings are thinking* !" (p.179 of Vol. 4 of the 1977 German edition.)

In the middle section, we learn that a form of soul-warmth is needed by the Archangels to uplift the incarnate human being's emotive-sensing life. The Exousiai and Kyriotetes are the beings who respond to this need. Since later, in the third section, the reference is to spiritual energies from the Earth, and its mineral crust, it is very likely that here, in the middle section, the needed soul-warmth, is from the planetary spheres.

In the last section, we learn that a spiritual power, from 'the Depths', is needed by the Archai to be able to exert their influences upon the inherent integrity of the incarnate human being's volition. The Kyriotetes, Dynameis, und Exousiai, are the beings who respond to this need. The entire verse is based on the World-cross or Cosmic-Cross; the heights above, the middle sphere in the horizontal plane, and then the depths below.

The spiritual energies needed by the Principalities or Archai are derived from that which has created, and now sustains, the mineral realm of the Earth.

The German text of VERSE for Lesson 19

Das Menschen-Ich weiß sich im Bereich des seraphisch-cherubinisch-Throne-getragenen Geistes-Worte

Der Hüter spricht aus der Ferne:
Wer spricht im Geistes-Wort
Mit der Stimme,
Die im Weltenfeuer lodert ?

(Aus dem Reich der ersten Hierarchie antwortet:)
Es sprechen Sternen-Flammen,
Es flammen seraph'sche Feuer-Mächte;

Sie flammen auch in meinem Herzen.
In des Urseins Liebe-Quell *   (*Götter-Quell)
Findet Menschen-Herz
Schaffendes Geistes-Flammen-Sprechen:
>   **Es ist Ich.**

Der Hüter spricht aus der Ferne:
Was denkt im Geistes-Wort
Mit Gedanken,
Die aus Weltenseelen bilden?

(Aus dem Reich der ersten Hierarchie antwortet:)
Es denken der Sterne Leuchter,
Es leuchten cherubin'sche Bilde-Kräfte;

Sie leuchten auch in meinem Haupte.
In des Urseins Lichtes-Quell
Findet Menschen-Haupt
Denkendes Seelen-Bilde-Wirken: (Seelen-Bilde-Weben)
>   **Es ist Ich.**

Der Hüter spricht aus der Ferne:
Was kraftet im Geistes-Wort
Mit Kräften,
Die im Weltenleibe leben?

(Aus dem Reich der ersten Hierarchie antwortet:)
Es kraftet der Sternen-Welten-Leib,
Es leiben der Throne Trag-Gewalten;

Sie leiben auch in meinen Gliedern.
In des Urseins Lebens-Quell *   (* Weltenleib)
Finden Menschen-Glieder
Kraftendes Welten-Träger-Walten:
>   **Es ist Ich.**

VERSE for Lesson 19

The human I knows itself in the realm of the Spirit-Word carried by seraphinic-cherubinic Thrones   1

The Guardian, from the distance:
Who is speaking in the Spirit-Word
with the voice that blazes forth in
the Fire of the Cosmos ?

From the realm of the 1st Hierarchy, answers:

Star-flames are speaking,   2
  Seraphinic Fire-Mights are flaming.

In the soul one feels:

They are aflame in my heart also;   3
in primal being's fountain of love *   4   (* fountain of gods)
human heart finds
creating flame-speaking of the spirit   5
  It is I

The Guardian, from the distance:
What is thinking in the Spirit Word   6
with thoughts which,   7
from out of the Souls of the Cosmos,   8
create forms ?

From the realm of the 1st Hierarchy, answers:

Star-illuminators are thinking,   9
Cherubinic form-shaping Powers are shining   10

In the soul one feels:

They are shining in my head, also.
In primal being's fountain of light,   10b
human head finds
cogitating form-shaping capacity of the soul: 11
  It is I

The Guardian, from the distance:
What is manifesting-in-strength* in the Spirit Word, (* 'powers')   12
With forces that live in the Body of the Cosmos ?   13

From the realm of the 1st Hierarchy, answers:

The stars' cosmic body is manifesting strength* (* 'is powering')   14
The Thrones' powers-of-sustaining   15
are becoming embodied   16

In the soul one feels:

They become embodied in my limbs, also.
In primal being's fountain of cosmic bodily life,   17
human limbs find
empowered prevailing of cosmic-body-bearers: 18
  It is I

Commentary: VERSE for Lesson 19 (page 1)

These last verses are particularly complex in their German form, showing the strain for an earthly language to become the bearer of such transcendent material.

1 "seraphinic-cherubinic Thrones": the common translations have *Seraphim, Cherubim and Thrones*, but this is incorrect. The German text informs us that the Thrones are the primary bearer of what the meditant perceives, but in this cosmic Word or resonance from the Thrones, there are discernible influences from the Cherubine and the Seraphine.

2 "Star-flames are speaking": the word ‚star' here is actually plural, = 'flames of the stars'.

3 "fountain of love": or, as written in Rudolf Steiner's notes; 'fountain of divine-beings'.

4 "Primal Being's ....": the usual version, 'the eternal fount...' is not helpful, being less accurate to the German. The core meaning of the entire verse is indicated in this phrase; i.e., the meditant has now a perception of higher Devachanic reality. And in this section, the meditant attains to some cognizance of the ancient primal devachanic Saturn Aeon conditions, wherein the Thrones manifested the 'fiery' ocean of the Atma, or Spirit-Man.

Note: this expression means 'primordial existence', rather than one specific ancient entity, but as the alternative version indicates, many gods are actually implied in this phrase: and this is also true of points 10b and 17, below.

5 "creative flame-speaking": this is accurate to the meaning. The meditant intuitively senses the divine basis of the core elements of human consciousness; in normal speaking, this is called 'sensing God'. It is not necessarily visual, but an inner experience of an ocean of divine 'fire'; a speaking from beings in the (non-radiant) star-strewn firmament.

6 "What is thinking?": this means in effect, 'What is cognizing-in-imagery', for it refers to the cosmic thought-forms produced by gods, which, as archetypes, have the forms of all created things. It does not refer to analytical thinking.

7 "thoughts": this refers to the radiant thought-forms of the gods' cosmic consciousness.

8 "from out of": (not just, 'from...') these additional words are to clarify the main point here, namely, that thoughts derive from the "cosmic-souls" (gods), and the great thought-forms forms, when used by the Cherubine, do have an inherently sculpturing, forming capacity. The translation, "with thoughts that are fashioning cosmic souls", reverses this meaning.

9 "Star-illuminators": the unusual German phrase means, 'that which lights up the stars', (their Devachanic aspect) hence more literally, 'the lighters of stars'. This refers to the activity of those Beings in the stars who generate the thought-forms which create the radiance of each star. This phrase can also mean, 'star torch-pole' or 'star torch'. In antiquity, a torch was a pole capped with cloth and dipped in oil, and then was set alight. Without this preparation, there would not be any flames to be a source of illumination. The Cherubine have a similar supportive role for the spiritual energies proceeding from the sublime Seraphine.

10 "form-shaping-Powers": this refers to thoughts which 'create forms', indicating the capacity to bring about images or spiritual forms (Devachanic or astral thought-forms) from which all things in the lower realms are created.

10b: "primal being": this expression means 'primordial existence', not a specific ancient entity entity, although as in #4's alternative version, many gods are implied in this. This phrase tells us that the Devachanic realms are being referred to.

Commentary: VERSE for Lesson 19 (page 2)

11 **"cogitating form-shaping capacity"** (or, form-making efficacy): this translation does accurately reflect the complex German phrase, which refers to the thinking capacity of the soul as something which creates forms or shapes (thought-forms). This capacity of making forms (thought-forms) which is inherent to our soul's capacity to think, is confirmed by an alternative version in a Rudolf Steiner notebook, "Seelen-Bilde-Weben", noted in the Archive (German) First Class book (vol. 4, p.135). This alternative version means 'the soul's ability to bring forth images', which is similar to "Seelen-Bilde-Wirken" (form-making capacity). In other words, just as the gods bring forth cosmic thought-forms or thought-images, from which they create all things, all of which have a shape, our soul forms mental pictures of all things (mental pictures or Vorstellungen). Further, there is the nuance here of the meditant attaining to higher consciousness and then experiencing their own capacity to intuitively perceive living images, from which objects are created. These images of course have a form or shape; this phrase is not pointing to thinking which, active in the soul, forms the soul itself, as suggested by the usual translations; ("thinking that works formatively in the soul").

12 **"Manifesting-in-strength"**: this third section refers to the will, and hence to the unfolding of an empowered, strong intentionality by the gods, from which physical creation itself derives, and our limbs, as organs of our will. In English it may be rendered as: what *'powers'* in the Spirit-word' ? But such an expression is scarcely permissible; so we would have to say, "what is 'powering' in the Spirit-word".

13 This entire line is pointing to the physical cosmos as the reflection of the Father-God's creative Will.

14 **"manifesting strength"**: as in line 12, the expression is literally "what is powering".

15 **"Powers-of-sustaining"**: or powers of upholding, or supporting.

16 **"becoming embodied"**: the actual English equivalent here would be the non-word 'bodifying', or as in some translations, 'bodys', as a verb.

17 **"fountain of cosmic bodily life"**: Rudolf Steiner wrote a different version, "Weltenleib", (cosmic body), in a notebook, instead of 'Lebensquell' (fountain of life). I have combined these two versions for completeness. (Erste Klasse, Vol 4, pp.135-6)

18 **"prevailing of cosmic-body-bearers"**: just as with Notes 11 & 17, a different version exists in a notebook to 'cosmic bearers' (Welten-Träger), namely "Leibes-Welten"; meaning 'cosmic body (bearers)'. For the sake of completeness, I have combined these two versions. Both of these phrases are referring to the great Thrones in the Saturn sphere. It is their task to support the cosmos on a subtle physical level. This task relates to their creativity in the Saturn Aeon when a tenuous, delicate physicality was created in the solar system, with the capacity to become, in a later aeon, the vessel for human will, through the limbs of the physical body. In this process, the Atma or Spirit-human is also being prepared; it hovers above our limb system, so to speak, (in German Archive First Class book (*Die Erste Klasse*, Vol 4, p. 137)

Developing the Higher-Self after death in Devachan

A brief text was published by the Rudolf Steiner Archives in 1969, as part of a book which made available hundreds of pages of material from Rudolf Steiner associated with the Mystery Dramas. This consists of sketches of scenes and outlines of themes, and also alternative speeches for characters in the four Dramas. These speeches were not actually used in the final versions of the Dramas. These unused versions often presented a different nuance or emphasis to those which were finally adopted, whilst other speeches were much more esoteric. The reason for a version not being included in the play is not recorded. The text we are contemplating here is a version of a speech for Maria, in Scene 9 of *The Souls' Awakening* (from GA 44, p. 421), which was not included. It is much more esoteric than the final version, and this may be the reason it was left out. It presents from high initiation wisdom a truly awe-inspiring secret about existence after death, for those who were actively on the esoteric path whilst in the body, seeking to meditate deeply, to develop their Spiritual-self, so that their consciousness can attain to Devachanic insights whilst incarnate.

It is normally understood from a study of Rudolf Steiner's works, that the Spiritual-self develops here on Earth, and that one cannot develop this after death of the body has occurred. (*My Rudolf Steiner Handbook* provides an overview of what we experience after death.) But this unused speech reveals that, for those who seek to enter the path of initiation to develop higher consciousness, it is actually possible to develop the Higher-self **after death** – that is, so long as one has self-awareness, a consciousness of self (although somewhat metamorphosed) in Devachan. It is significant here to note that Rudolf Steiner once defined the purpose of anthroposophy as, to help souls awaken in Devachan.

The tremendous revelation in this speech concerns how one develops the Spiritual-self, (and, possibly, also an incipient Life-Spirit), in the Midnight Hour after death. The location of this point appears to be the Saturn sphere. The speech is given first, followed by an expanded version of this, with commentary.

The Souls' Awakening (Der Seelen Erwachen)

An alternative, unused, version of a speech by Maria, for Scene 9.

Maria: In cosmic light the Word is empowered
which was entrusted to me at the cosmic midnight.
Remembrance vivifies this spiritual-word by fire of will
so that it endures in temporal existence.
In earthly life it now continues to resound to me.
In its resonance, my higher cognizing returns
to me from spirit heights, with my Self.
For me, my higher cognizing is existing with my Self.
At the cosmic midnight, my higher cognizing created
for me out of rays of spirit light, the Self.
The Self in which the flames are ignited,
which are permitted to shine as far as the shore of the soul.
In the temporal-flow the guide often spoke, and
in his word Eternity resounded.
In me it experiences only the present time.
The cosmic midnight shines into the present time
with the light of time-distanced Eternity –
the wise guide gave the power to the
temporal-word which created for my Self
the impetus of will to behold with him
the cosmic Midnight Hour.

(See below for the German original)

Commentary and expanded version of the speech by Maria

Earlier scenes had depicted for the audience, Maria's earlier life in 14th Europe, as a monk, and then in later scenes, her life long ago in Egypt is depicted, where she was an acolyte in a temple (probably at Thebes), and underwent an unorthodox initiation experience. All of this forms a background to her 20th century incarnation, as a student of anthroposophical wisdom. In this unused speech, she is having an experience wherein she recollects, livingly, her journey into the spiritual worlds after her death in the 14th century; in particular her sojourn in the Saturn-sphere. Maria now, in the 20th century, has an extraordinary clairvoyant experience:

> In cosmic light the Word is empowered
> which was entrusted to me at the Cosmic Midnight.

At this moment of higher clairvoyant experience, Maria becomes aware of the cosmic experience that she had experienced after her last death when she was in the Saturn sphere; a realm which correlates to the third level of Devachan. She was aware of a cosmic resonance, which is described as being 'empowered'. So as her meditation enables here to recall her time in Devachan, this previous experience is recalled, and in that sense, it now has a stronger presence in her.

> Remembrance vivifies this Spiritual-Word by fire of will
> so that it endures in temporal existence.
> In earthly life it now continues to resound to me.

This recalling is a recollection of her time in the spiritual world after her death; it can be seen as partly the outcome of *Practising Spirit-remembering* (*Übe Geist-Erinnern*) mentioned in the Foundation Stone Meditation. The spiritualized will-forces within her now empowers this resonance in such a way that it continues to be present to her mind whilst she is incarnate.

> In its resonance my higher cognizing
> {*which I had in the Cosmic Midnight Hour*}
> returns to me, from spirit heights, with my Self.

In the actual experiencing of this resonance, her higher spiritual awareness returns; her Higher-self ! It returns as she is aware, from Devachan – and brings with it, her Self: that is, her Spiritual-Self ! This development means that a well-known general meditation from Rudolf Steiner no longer applies in her case:

> I gaze into the darkness; in it there arises Light,
> living light. Who is this light in the darkness?
> I myself am it - in my reality. This reality of the I
> enters not into my earthly life. I am but an image of this.
> But I shall find it again when with good will for the spirit
> I have passed through the portal of death.

Because, as Maria now affirms:

> For me, my higher cognizing is {*now*} existing with my {higher-} Self.

That is, the 'higher cognizing' is the Spiritual-self, which is now permeating her **current** 20th century self. Her everyday ego is in union with her higher, eternal Self.
This earthly ego is **becoming** this higher eternal Self.
She proceeds to analyse, or to intuit, what all this implies.

> At the Cosmic Midnight my higher cognizing created

the Self for me, out of rays of spirit light.

The tremendous revelation here is that, during her conscious cognizing after death, in a state of Devachanic awareness, this cognizing by Maria **created this Higher Self**, from rays of spiritual light emanating from the Hierarchies. These rays of divine light may have emanated from the Thrones, who rule the Saturn sphere.

Now, when we recall that the foremost of the Thrones is the Father-God, at least in the first instance, then the sublime nature of the experience by Maria is glimpsed by us. For Maria was experiencing "God" in her existence, in Devachan after her life in the 14th century. So here the profound Rosicucian motto is becoming an existential truth for her, but on a higher level than is normally understood, or would apply to non-initiated human beings:

Ex Deo Nascimur - from God we are born.

This is the birth hour of the eternal Higher Self. So this is another process through which the Higher Self is created; bringing to completion, or extending, the other, better known process, which occurs whilst the acolyte is incarnate; that is, through the meditative initiatory path.

> The Self in which the flames are ignited, which
> are permitted to shine as far as the shore of the soul.

The Higher-self contains spiritual Devachanic radiance, and this is now permitted to permeate the earthly soul. The first of the two Devachanic auras is now developing well. As I pointed out in *The Way to The Sacred*, our Higher-self consists of the Devachanic 'body' or aura of the Spiritual-self, and also a second aura or another Devachanic 'body', in which the Life-spirit and Spirit-human exist.

> In the temporal-flow the Guide often spoke, and
> in his word Eternity resounded.

In the 20th century, Benedictus often advised Maria, and in his esoteric teaching, Devachanic reality resounded.

> In me it* experiences only the present time, {*but now....*}

In her, the Word from Benedictus ("it") only experiences a current personality; it does not find resonances of an eternalized ego with Maria. But in view of what is being said in this speech, it appears that through the body-language of the actress, it would become apparent to the audience that, although the Word (that is, the instruction from Benedictus) was not received at first, by an eternalized ego in Maria, this is no longer the case. Because as she speaks further, Maria tells us that she is now experiencing his teachings, with her Higher-self having a presence within her sense of self.

> The Cosmic Midnight shines into the present time
> with the light of time-distanced Eternity –

Now the memory of the Saturn-sphere experience is shining into her current personality:

> The wise Guide gave that power to the temporal-word

{back in the 14th century incarnation, when the monk was taught in visions, by the great Benedictus, who had been Thomas Aquinas, who was by now deceased.}

which created for my Self
the impetus of Will to behold {*consciously*}
with him the {*cosmic Word resounding in the*} Cosmic Midnight Hour,
{*after her death as a monk in the 14th century –*
an experience which she now, in the 20th century is recalling}.

Benedictus as her guide in the 20th century had imbued his words with Devachanic depth, and this allowed her, just a few months ago, to recall, in the company of Benedictus, that time long ago, during her journey after her death in the 14th century, as her medieval lifetime ended, when she was in the Saturn-sphere; Maria was then already able to consciously experience her environs. And in having the capacity to be self-conscious in this sphere, she was able to undergo the sublime, glorious experience of hearing the Word of the divine-spiritual beings. As this reciprocal interweaving of her soul-spirit self occurred, her Spiritual-self began to form much more powerfully; it was no longer just germinal.

Goethe's Fairy Tale of the Green Snake and the Beautiful Lily

We can contrast this revelation with the teaching of Rudolf Steiner that in the after-life existence, although the non-spiritualizing soul does have some cognizance of the divine-spiritual Hierarchies, their sublime resonance is perceived only vaguely by such souls, as a kind of faint background noise.

A brief text in the inspired fairy-tale by Johann W. von Goethe, *The Fairy Tale of the Green Snake and the Beautiful Lily*, refers to this possibility. The Green snake (the somewhat spiritualizing earthly-self) is in conversation with its potential Spiritual-self (the Golden King).

The dialogue between the Green Snake and the Gold King proceeds as follows:

Gold King: "Where do you come from?"

Green Snake: "From the crevices where the gold dwells."
(Gold represents wisdom, and the earthly self arises from being incarnate; it is meant to seek for wisdom in the earthly world.)

Gold King: "What is more glorious than gold?"

Green Snake: "Light."
(Gold derives from etheric solar light, and wisdom from spiritual light, emanating from the Gods.)

Gold King: "What is more animating than light?"

Green Snake: "Conversation."
(The dialogue or conversation of the Gods the thoughts of the Gods, moving in a living interweaving with one another, causes the sublime radiance in Devachan.)

How many students of anthroposophical wisdom, at sometime in the future, as they recall their journey into spiritual realms, after after the 20-21st century incarnation, shall have this experience; perhaps around the 30th century AD? A significant question to ponder.

The German text of Maria's speech

Es ist in Weltenlicht das Wort erkraftet,

Das mir zur Weltenmitternacht vertraut {war}.

Erinnerung belebt am Willensfeuer

Mit Zeitendauerkraft das Weltenwort.

Im Erdenleben tönt es mir nun fort.

In seinem Tönen kommt mein Denken mir,

Mit meinem Selbst aus Geisteshöhn zurück.

Es lebt mein Denken - mir - mit meinem Selbst −

Zur Weltenmitternacht erschuf mein Denken

Aus Geisteslichtesstrahlen mir das Selbst:

Das Selbst, in dem die Flamme sich entzündet,

Die bis zum Seelenufer leuchten darf − −

Im Zeitenlaufe sprach der Führer oft,

In seinem Worte klang die Ewigkeit −

In mir erlebt es nur die Gegenwart.

Die Weltenmitternacht erstrahlt der Gegenwart

Im Licht der zeitenfernen Ewigkeit − −

 (*Benedictus tritt ein*)

Der Weise Führer gab dem Zeitenwort die Kraft,

Die meinem Selbst die Willenschwungen schufen,

Mit ihm die Weltenmitternacht zu schaun.

(from GA 44, p. 421).

1 Doré's woodcut of "the Empyrean" from Dante's Divine Comedy

Appendix

The Luciferic and Ahrimanic Doubles

When meditation is carried out over years, then what Rudolf Steiner terms "Imagination" arises; this clairvoyant state can also be called Psychic-Image consciousness. In this state, etheric and astral realities begin to be perceived. At first, this new, higher 'thinking' (as Rudolf Steiner would refer to it) is only a delicate, subtle experience. One result of this state is to see 'faces' everywhere, formed by the contours of everyday objects around one. One also sees the beautiful phenomena of etheric forces actively or gently permeating the air and plant life. Rudolf Steiner gently drew attention to this in a conversation with the artist Assia Turgenieff. As I reported in *The Way to the Sacred*, Rudolf Steiner spoke briefly to her of this phenomenon, "Nature strives everywhere to make faces. That is its goal. And when I go outside, I constantly see faces, which are trying to come into being, everywhere..."[20] (He gave no explanation of this phenomenon.)

Such etheric shapes imprint themselves subtly onto physical forms, being only just discernible, at the edge of our awareness. This phenomenon of an etheric form discreetly overlaid onto a physical form, is also affirmed in another private conversation which Rudolf Steiner had with a student. This person was Guenther Wachsmuth, who reports that in the air over some parts of Germany, the clouds would at times seem to have the form of long-extinct animals (presumably dinosaurs). Rudolf Steiner confirmed that these apparent shapes were in fact genuinely reflecting etheric forms; the clouds were making manifest the shape of ancient animals. One concludes from these remarks that the shapes of the extinct animals persisted on in the ethers, influencing cloud-forms even on in modern times. These animals may have existed as etheric forms, not as physical forms.

The wooden statue "the Representative of Humanity" on its physical level, is a wondrous achievement, which we won't be describing in detail here. Briefly, it depicts in its centre, the figure of Jesus Christ at the moment of the Resurrection. It also depicts Lucifer and Ahriman in two separate forms: before the Resurrection of Christ and after this event. These two fallen beings are working in together, and are placed in the left and middle part of the statue. But on the far right, partly obscured, is Lucifer, now falling from his proud status, and also Ahriman is depicted as bound and weakened, inside the Earth. There is also on the upper far left, a smiling being; this was added later in the process of making the statue. When asked about this being, Rudolf Steiner replied that it was a kind of elemental entity or 'rock-being', who was bemused at the statue. He was not obliged to reveal any more about the deep, stern mystery that the statue contains, aided by this this little sprite's features. He did also comment that it was linked to a cosmic humour quality. On a deeper level, it helps to shape a hidden etheric form (see below).

In fact he commented on one occasion that he was not permitted to present the true forms of the lower nature of humanity (the Luciferic and Ahrimanic Doubles) because humanity could not bear to see this.[21] It is due to this situation, that this statue contains a mystery, which until now has not been seen. Rudolf Steiner was aware that people need to encounter the sight of their twofold lower qualities, yet, because this is generally too strong an experience for humanity, the decision was made to reveal these two Doubles in a discreet way, a way which would also partially conceal them.

This complex carving, nearly 10 metres high, has not only physical depictions; it also has veiled etheric depictions. I have decided to reveal this etheric hidden side of the

[20] Reported by Assia Turgenieff, in "Erinnerungen an Rudolf Steiner" (Vlg Freies Geistesleben; Stuttgart, 1972), p. 99.
[21] ref. 20

statue, even if in an obscure way, because of the damage done to the intentions of Rudolf Steiner with regard to this statue. His intention was that it be placed at the back of the stage of the Goetheanum; in this way, the soul would be discreetly informed about the grim subject of their own Luciferic and Ahrimanic Doubles. Then people, gazing at the stage, on any occasion, would have perceived, subconsciously, perhaps semi-consciously, these two images. Those who take the time to contemplate the following images, will find that the outline of the 'rock sprite' provides a vital part of the Luciferic Double's appearance. This is an invaluable, but confronting lesson in self-knowledge; Rudolf Steiner knew that this is a lesson which Higher Powers decreed human beings needed to have.

This profound intention was thwarted with regard to the first Goetheanum because of the arson in early 1924, which destroyed this building. It is regrettable that Rudolf Steiner's intention for the placement of the statue in the second Goetheanum, in the Great Hall, was not carried out. It was placed instead in a smallish cavity, far from the eyes of anyone who entered the Great Hall. In its present cavity, it can be viewed up close, but not seen in its entirety, and not from a distance – yet it is precisely the distant view of the entire statue which is needed, to allow the etheric forms of the horrendous beings to be perceived; they cannot be seen when one is up close, near to the statue.

It is my sincere hope that, in pointing out the existence of these subtle images, and thereby making them more accessible, that this may assist the thwarted intentions of Rudolf Steiner regarding this great carving, with its hidden etheric scene.

The two images which follow that of the complete statue, are quite small and also a little unclear, because considerable discretion in this matter is called for.

2 The Representative of Man sculpture:
wood, 10 metres in height, its finer details were not completed.

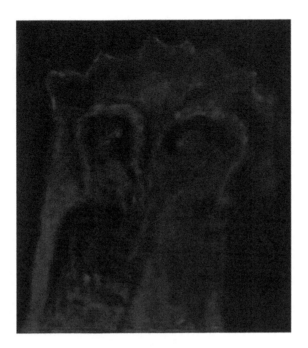

3 The Luciferic Double: sensuality, vanity, conceited attitudes, blind self-love, spiteful acts: and (in conjunction with Ahriman), vindictive jealously, vicious lusts and unplanned acts of vengeance.

© Adrian Anderson 2019   Copying or distribution of this image is prohibited.

4 The Ahrimanic Double: dead thinking, cold, unfeeling arrogance, rigid, narrow attitudes, callous indifference, cold hatred, cruelty, planned heinous crimes.

© Adrian Anderson 2019   Copying or distribution of this image is prohibited.

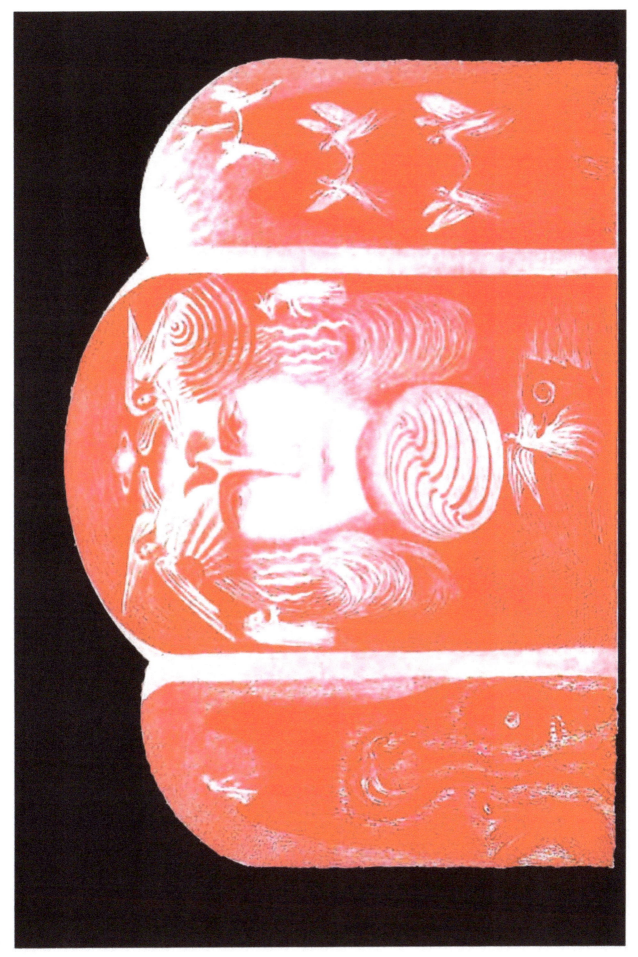

It manifests   I am beholding   It has manifested

6 The 3 Beasts, as depicted in the Red Window of the Goetheanum.
(Depicted in red, but they are coloured here to show the qualities mentioned in the verse.)
Left: Doubt, in the thinking: a bird so earth-bound, it cannot soar aloft.
Middle: Fear, in the will; a skeletal creature without the spirit: animal will-forces.
Right: Hate, in the emotions; deadened intellectuality from feelings denying of the spirit.

7 Light and Darkness: Pastel drawing from Rudolf Steiner, March 1923.
It depicts, upper left, the Luciferic influence, radiating out in vermilion tones, manifesting in the human countenance; nuances of immaturity and self-focus, mixed with idealism. Lower right is the Ahrimanic influence, self-contained in sombre bluish tones: there are nuances of rigidity and coldness, heartless calculating, self-interested intentions.

8 Elemental beings: a pastel drawing by Rudolf Steiner, November 1923.
We are looking down a river; floating in the (not-visible) water are several undines, emerging
out of the ground. Near a bush on the river-bank are some gnomes. In the blue sky are three
sylphs, near two birds; and higher up, near some butterflies, are two pyraustas (fire-sprites).
On the left is an Ahrimanic face, on the right a Luciferic face, indicating that these elementals,
including fallen ones, exert an influence in human beings.

9 **The Stuttgart Zodiac** (1912-1937) The new images here are contemplations on the significance of the zodiac energies for humanity's evolution. (There is an additional Aquarian Age symbol, see the author's *The Lost Zodiac of Rudolf Steiner*, for more about this zodiac.)

*And the Spirit of Heaviness gathered the resistance and
there developed opposition in the human will.*

The will is being born   *The world actively effects my will*   *The will is {now} born*

GLOSSARY of some central anthroposophical terms

aeon: a long evolutionary phase. There are seven of these, and we are now in the fourth such epoch. They are the Saturn, Sun, Moon, Earth (which has two halves, Mars and Mercury) Jupiter, Venus and Vulcan aeons.

Ahriman: an evil entity responsible for the attitude which sees matter as the only thing in creation, denying spiritual reality. It correlates to the Biblical term, Satan.

Angels: spiritual beings who are one aeon ahead of human beings in the evolution.

anthroposophy: a Greek word that literally means 'human-soul wisdom'. In Rudolf Steiner's usage it means the wisdom that can dawn in a person's consciousness, in their spiritual-soul; and which fully manifests when the Spirit-self is developed.

Archangels: spiritual beings who are two aeons ahead of human beings in the evolution.

astral body: the soul, seen as an aura around the body.

astral realm: the Soul-world, above the ethers, but below the Devachanic realms.

astrality: soul energies, but often it refers mainly to the feelings.

Buddhi Plane: a realm more transcendent than Devachan; where the Bodhisattvas exist

Consciousness-soul: (see spiritual-soul)

Cosmic Christ: the highest of the 'Powers' or sun-gods.

Devachan: the true heavens above the Soul-world; a Theosophical term from the Sanskrit meaning 'realm of the shining gods'; it is the realm of the archetypal Idea of Plato.

the Double: a term usually referring to the Lower Self.

ego or self or I: the sense of self, but the eternal self is linked to this. Hence the ego is a dual or twofold thing.

egoism or egoistic: not quite the same as the well-known term egotism (which means conceit). Egoism is used by Rudolf Steiner to mean either the state of having a normal earth-centred ego, or for this earthly sense of self behaving in a selfish way.

etheric body: is made of the four ethers and duplicates the physical body's appearance, from which organic matter, such as new cells, are condensed.

ethers: subtle energies which sustain all living things on the Earth. Electricity and magnetism are formed as they decompose.

Group-soul: a spirit-being to whom all the animals of a particular species belong.

intellectual-soul: the rational, logical capacity.

Imagination, Inspiration, Intuition: Latin words for the three types of clairvoyance, but which mean something different in everyday usage in English to the meanings that Rudolf Steiner gives them.

Imagination: the first stage of clairvoyance; can be called 'Psychic-Image consciousness'. It brings perception of astral or etheric images, (usually means 'fantasy'.)

Imaginations: astral thought-forms. Inspiration: this can be called 'Cosmic-Spiritual consciousness', it is a perceiving or

'breathing-in' wisdom, from lower Devachan. (In normal English usually this word means a strongly felt creative urge or idea.)

Intuition: this can be called a 'High Initiation consciousness'. It is a perceiving or inwardly becoming one with another being. This state allows the seer to perceive at an upper Devachan level. (In normal English this word usually means a semi-psychic awareness of something.)

intuition: can be used by Rudolf Steiner for the above high seership, but can sometimes appear in English anthroposophical texts in its usual English meaning of 'insights' (translating such German words as 'ahnen').

life-force: an alternative term for ether.

life-force organism: the ether body.

Life-spirit: the divinized etheric body, is made of Devachanic energies.

lower-self: the soul qualities that are tainted with Luciferic or Ahrimanic influences. It can be thought of as threefold, the lower thinking, feeling and will. But Rudolf Steiner also described it as sevenfold, being the lower qualities of the seven classical planets in astrology.

Lucifer: a 'fallen' entity who opposes the intentions of the higher gods, creating an ungrounded, naïve attitude in human beings, but also instils a sense of self and enthusiasm for beauty, art and sensuality.

sentient-soul: the feelings, the emotion capacities of the soul.

soul: appears as an aura, and contains the sentient-soul, intellectual-soul and spiritual-soul.

Spirit-human: the divine forces underlying the physical body, in our subconscious will.

Spirit-self: the result of the purified and enlightened threefold soul-body or astral body.

Spiritual-self: alternative name for the Spirit-self.

spiritual-soul: also translated as 'consciousness soul', and could be called the intuitive
or   soul. This is the soul capacity which underlies intuitive decision-making or
spirit-soul   intuitive flashes of insight. But it is also the most individualized or 'ego-ic'
                soul capacity, and can tend towards a hardened self-centredness.

Spiritual-sun: the sun on its soul (or astral) level, behind the physical globe, and also on its actual spiritual level (also referred to as the Devachanic level): these levels comprise many energies and divine beings.

thinking: can be used to mean the exercise of our intelligence, but it is also used to mean any of the three clairvoyant states we can attain.

Further books by Adrian Anderson

Living a Spiritual Year: seasonal festivals in both hemispheres	1992
(new, expanded edition, 2016)	
The Way to the Sacred	2003
The Foundation Stone Meditation: a new commentary	2005
Dramatic Anthroposophy: Identification and contextualization of primary features of Rudolf Steiner's anthroposophy. (PhD thesis)	2005
Two Gems from Rudolf Steiner	2014
The Hellenistic Mysteries & Christianity	2014
Rudolf Steiner Handbook	2014
Horoscope Handbook – a Rudolf Steiner Approach	2015
The Meaning of the Goetheanum Windows	2016
Rudolf Steiner's Esoteric Christianity in the Grail painting by Anna May	2017
The Vidar Flame Column – its meaning from Rudolf Steiner	2017
Blessed: Rudolf Steiner on the Beatitudes	2018

See also as Damien Pryor:

The nature & origin of the Tropical Zodiac	2011
Stonehenge	2011
The Externsteine	2011
Lalibela	2011
The Great Pyramid & the Sphinx	2011

Website: www.rudolfsteinerstudies.com

This site has information on all of these books, as well as free downloads of various essays, and a link to the author's ARTPRINTS page, which offers esoteric diagrams and great classical works of art which are relevant to the understanding of anthroposophy. If you wish to contribute to the furthering of this work, there is an opportunity through the Donate page.